WHAT THE ENEMY TOOK

I AM TAKING IT BACK

THE LINE OF RECOVERY

DR. ONIKA CAMPBELL ROWE

TABLE OF CONTENTS

What The 1

Enemy Took 1

I Am Taking It Back 1

The Line Of Recovery 1

Dr. Onika Campbell Rowe 1

Preface 1

The Fire Didn't Come To Consume You — It Came To Refine You 1

When Evil Felt Like It Won 3

The Power Of Spiritual Grounding 4

This Fire Doesn't Burn — It Builds 4

This Is An Altar. 6

...Dem Affi Pay! Meaning, There Is No Escaping The Wrath Of God! 6

Inspiration From My Niece And Son 7

With Love And Admiration, ... 8

My Friend, ... 9

    Unveiling The Tactics Of The Enemy 10

    Identifying The Signs Of Theft And Loss 14

What The Enemy Silenced, God Is Reviving 17

You've Been Quiet For Too Long 17

Get Back Your Voice 18

    Subheading: The Roar Of The Redeemed 18

    Real-Life Story: Dana's Silenced Prayers 19

Get Back Your Vow 20

    Realign With Your First Yes 20

    Your Moment: 21

Get Back Your Victory 22

    The Battle Is Already Won — Walk In It 22

The Quiet Comeback 23

Activations 24

. Decree To Take Back Your Voice: 24

Recommit Your Vow To God: 25

You're Not Powerless — You're Positioned 26

Understanding The Spirit Of Deception 28

Biblical Foundations Of Restoration 33

    God's Promises To Restore What Was Taken 34

    Faith Anchors In Times Of Loss 35

    Jesus' Example Of Recovery And Victory 38

3// Confronting Pain And Disappointment 42

    Honoring Your Feelings With Integrity 43

Choosing Forgiveness Over Offense 45

Healing Through God's Comfort 48

4// Decree And Declaration: Reclaiming What Is Rightfully Yours 52

The Power Of Spoken Faith 53

Scriptural Declarations For Recovery 56

Creating Your Personal Warfare Script 59

5// The Strategies Of Spiritual Warfare 62

Binding And Loosing In The Spirit 62

Utilizing Prayer As A Weapon 65

The Authority Of The Believer 69

6// Breaking Generational And Soul Ties 72

Identifying Unhealthy Spiritual Bonds 72

Renouncing And Releasing With Authority 76

How To Enforce God's Promises Like A Legal Right 80

The Courtroom Of Heaven Is Not Moved By Tears — It's Moved By Truth 80

Spiritual Law Vs. Emotional Release 81

The Real-Life Turnaround 82

Act Of Activation 83

Keys To Enforcing Spiritual Law 84

Encouragement 85

Faith Is What Plants It — Expectation Is What Grows It 86

Biblical Principle 87

Real-Life Connection 88

Declaration Time 89

    Embracing Holiness And Identity In Christ 90

7. Faith-Based Restoration Processes 94

    Aligning Your Faith With God's Word 94

    Practicing Patience And Expectancy 97

    Testimonies Of Divine Repair 100

8. Rebirthing Confidence And Self-Worth 104

    Replacing Lies With God's Truth 104

    Building A Strong Inner Identity 107

    Walking In Discernment And Authority 108

9. Overcoming Fear, Doubt, And Insecurity 112

    Tearing Down Strongholds Of Fear 112

    Renewing The Mind With Scripture 115

    Stepping Out In Bold Faith 118

10. Aligning With Kingdom Principles For Recovery 123

    Stewardship And Faithfulness 123

Chapter Four: Double For Your Trouble 128

    You Paid A Price No One Saw 128

The Compensation Season Has Arrived 130

Biblical Foundation: The Job Story 131

Real-Life Story: Vanessa's Ministry Loss Led To Global Expansion 132

Why The Oil Is Expensive 133

    The Double Comes With A Purpose 133

Supporting Scriptures For Your Season Of Double 134

    Declare This Over Yourself Now: 134

Activation: Prepare For The Overflow 135

Closing Word 136

    Generosity As A Recovery Tool 137

    God Is Not Denying You — He's Aligning You 141

    She Should've Been Married By Now. 141

    Delay Feels Like Rejection, But It's Often Protection. 142

    When Delay Is Spiritual, Only Spiritual Weapons Can Break It 143

    The Delay Wasn't Denial — It Was Interception 145

    Recognizing The Spirit Of Delay 146

    God's Verdict Is: Time's Up 147

    Scripture Breakthroughs 148

    Prayer Of Breakthrough 149

Activation Time: Write The Delay Down — Then Break It 150

    Encouragement: 151

    Walking In Obedience And Discipline 152

11. Navigating Emotional And Spiritual Breakthroughs 154

    Recognizing When Breakthrough Has Begun 154

    Maintaining The Breakthrough Momentum 157

    Giving God All The Glory 160

12. Reclaiming Your Destiny And Purpose 165

    Rediscovering God's Call For Your Life 165

From **Betrayal, Envy, Emotional Pain, Ungratefulness, Deceit To Spiritual Grounding, Vindication, And Triumphant Promotion**, Centered Around A **True-To-Life Story**, Grounded In **Scripture**, And Built For **Healing, Inspiration, And Fire-Filled Restoration**. 168

    This Is Repayment With Interest 170

    Let This Be Your Declaration: 171

Get Back Activation 172

    Let's Break That Down Spiritually: 172

    Overcoming Past Failures And Setbacks 174

    Stepping Into God's Greater Plan 177

    Heaven Has A Strategy For Your Comeback 181

    Breakthrough Doesn't Happen By Accident — It Happens By Alignment 181

    A Word For The Weary 182

    Recovery Is Always Tied To A Prophetic Act. 183

    Protocol #1: Ask God For A Recovery Word 183

Protocol #2: Break Agreement With Loss 184

Protocol #3: Move In Faith-Filled Action 185

Protocol #4: Sow Where You Want To Go 186

Protocol #5: Guard Your Gate 187

Real-Life Testimony: How Lisa Reclaimed Her Family 188

Your Prophetic Recovery Checklist 189

Declare This Boldly: 190

Final Word 191

13. Building A Support System Of Faith And Encouragement ... 192

Connecting With Like-Minded Believers 192

Betrayed But Not Broken. 196

God Will Use What Cuts You To Crown You 196

You Never Saw It Coming 196

The Weight Of Betrayal 198

Jesus Understands Betrayal 199

God Will Use What Cuts You To Crown You 200

Personal Story: Kell Betrayal Became Her Breakthrough 201

Betrayal Is A Door — Not A Death Sentence 204

Signs That You're Healing From Betrayal 205

Activation Time 206

Action: Let It Go, So You Can Grow 207

Encouragement 208

    Accountability And Prayer Partners.......................................209

    Leveraging Testimony For Empowerment..............................212

14. Maintaining Victory Through Worship And Prayer............................216

    Worship As Warfare 216

    Consistent Prayer And Supplication 219

    Staying Vigilant Spiritually 222

15. Walking In Continual Victory And Faith 226

    Developing A Lifestyle Of Declaration....................................226

    Avoiding Backsliding And Complacency 229

    Living As A Conqueror In Christ..233

You Survived The War Because You Were Chosen For The Reward237

    You Didn't Just Come Through — You Came Out Crowned......237

    You Made It. 238

    What Is The Reward?..239

    You Didn't Lose — You Were Planted..240

Declaration: The Reward Is Yours..241

    Instructions:..242

Your Journey Has Just Begun...243

Final Blessing Over You:...244

    What The Enemy Took!..244

The Reward Is Yours. 244

The Last Teardrop And The Rescue – Vindication At Last 246

   The Ones I Helped… 246

   Betrayal Is A Cross, Not A Curse 248

   I Lied On The Floor In Tears — But I Got Up In Fire 249

   Now The Fire Burns Within Me 250

   Ungratefulness Is Worse Than Obeah 251

   Promotion Is Here — Not In Spite Of The Fire, But Because Of It 252

   Final Prophetic Decree Over Your Life: 253

   This Is Not Just A Book — It's A Resurrection 254

   Scriptures For Your Sealing Season: 255

   Closing Charge: 256

About The Author 257

A Mission-Driven Global Voice 258

   Champion Of Affordable Education 263

   Other Works By The Author: 264

PREFACE

The Fire Didn't Come to Consume You, It Came to Refine You

This book was not born in comfort.

It was born in betrayal.

In sleepless nights.

 In whispered prayers. In broken trust. In silent screams behind closed doors. It was written between boardroom betrayals and ministry heartbreaks…

Between helping hands turned hostile…

Between God's silence and the enemy's laughter.

I didn't write this to be poetic.

I wrote this because I *survived* what should've destroyed or killed me.

What do you do when the very people you fed turn around and feed lies about you?

When those you mentored begin to mimic you, not to honor, but to **replace** you?

When your name is dragged by the very mouths you prayed for?

When your business is sabotaged by someone you once called family?

I'll tell you what I did:

I bled quietly.

I cried privately.

And then, I broke… not down, but open.

This book is not just a memoir — it's a **manual for the broken that are still called.**

It's for every leader who's been lied to, every entrepreneur who's been copied and cut out, every minister who poured oil into someone who turned around and used it to burn them.

It's for *you*, beloved — the one who knows what it feels like to have your kindness mistaken for weakness and your silence mistaken for guilt.

You didn't deserve the betrayal, but you were chosen to overcome it.

This is the story of **how I got my voice back**,

How I **reclaimed my vow**,

And how I **walked into vindication without ever throwing a punch.**

When Evil Felt Like It Won

There came a moment when I had to wrestle with heaven:

"God, how could You allow this? I honored you. I loved them. I obeyed. So why… this?"

And then came the whisper:

"Daughter, I didn't let them win. I let them expose themselves.

Because where I'm taking you, they can't follow."

That changed everything.

I realized I was not being *punished*.

I was being *processed*.

Refined for promotion.

Prepared for the purpose.

Being set apart, not cast aside.

God was never absent. He was **architecting a divine reset** — even when I thought I was being ruined.

The Power of Spiritual Grounding

Every chapter in this book is backed by the Word of God.

Because when betrayal came, it wasn't motivational quotes that kept me—it was **Scripture**.

I didn't stand on emotions—I stood on **spiritual law**.

The Word grounded me when lies swirled.

It anchored me when shame tried to suffocate me.

And it rebuked every demon of delay, deception, and discouragement that came against me.

I became one with the Spirit—not just in praise, but in pain.

And in the darkest hour… the **fire came.**

This Fire Doesn't Burn — It Builds

Now I burn with truth.

With authority.

With clarity.

With holy fire.

Not revenge.

Not bitterness.

But *righteous indignation and restored identity*.

I know who I am — and this book will help you remember who **you** are, too.

You are not crazy.

You are not alone.

And you are not finished.

This is an altar.

And every page is a **sacrifice of pain turned into praise.**

So read slowly.

Weep if you must.

Highlight. Pray. Declare.

Then rise with the fire that now burns within you.

Because what the enemy took… God is giving back, and this time, with interest.

…Dem Affi Pay! Meaning, there is no escaping the wrath of God!

Inspiration From my Niece and Son

Dear Auntie Kel,

I finally got the chance to finish your book, and honestly... I'm blown away. It's so powerful. I could feel every word. It didn't just read like a book; it felt like you were talking straight to my heart.

One part that really stuck with me was when you said, "I bled quietly. I cried privately. And then, I broke... not down, but open." That hit me deeply. I've had moments like that myself, and reading how you turned all that pain into purpose gave me so much hope.

I also loved the story about Dana, the worship leader who lost her voice after everything she went through. It reminded me that no matter how much we've lost, God can still use us. That line, "Your mouth births miracles," really made me pause and reflect. It's a reminder that even in brokenness, there's still so much power and purpose.

Thank you for writing this. It's not just inspiring, it's healing. I honestly feel stronger after reading it. It reminded me that even when life knocks us down, we can still rise up and take back everything the enemy tried to steal.

I'm so proud of you, Auntie. And I'm incredibly honored to be one of the few who got to read this beautiful piece of work before it's published. I just know this book is going to bless and transform so many lives, just like it did mine.

With love and admiration,

Kimaya

Hello Mom,

This is a divine awakening for your soul; you've been silent and spiritually muted, but your voice and authority are being restored. The enemy's lies disguised as partial truths have tried to distort your identity and diminish your faith. But God's Word is your weapon. By declaring His promises and renewing your vow, you reclaim your power, your joy, and your victory. Your voice is coming back, stronger than ever. Your victory is non-negotiable. Rise, speak, and reclaim what's rightfully yours because your spiritual authority is being restored by divine decree.

-Danteyo

My Friend,

In the wild, the dog barks loudly.

Echoes of freedom rise from the crowd.

Waves of laughter roll like the sea.

In the dance of life, I choose to be free.

With every step, my heart takes flight.

Embracing the day, igniting the night.

No looking back, no stones to cast.

Forward is where my spirit is vast.

Bradley Burke

Figure 1.1

Unveiling the Tactics of the Enemy

Understanding the tactics of the enemy begins with recognizing that his primary goal is to undermine your confidence in God's promises and to sow discord within your soul. Often, he operates subtly, weaving into your thoughts feelings of doubt, worthlessness, and despair that seem almost automatic. He specializes in planting seeds of confusion and fears, making you question your identity in Christ and the purpose God has for you.

When you become aware that these attacks are not random but strategic, it becomes easier to see through his plans and stand against them. Awareness is a spiritual gift that aligns your heart to discern the enemy's schemes, enabling you to resist and reclaim what has been stolen.

Beyond recognizing these tactics, it's essential to understand that the enemy often targets your weakest points—areas where you feel vulnerable or wounded. He takes advantage of moments when you're exhausted, hurt, or grieving, amplifying feelings of abandonment or betrayal. Sometimes, he whispers lies that twist reality, convincing you that your pain is permanent or that your recovery is impossible. Other times, he uses discouragement to drown out hope, convincing you to give up on your dreams and on God's faithful promises. By staying alert to these patterns, you can begin to see his manipulations clearly, breaking the hold of these lies and standing firm in your faith and identity in Christ.

It's also crucial to remember that these strategies are not new or unique to you. The scriptures reveal that Satan has been scheming from the beginning, using deception as his most powerful weapon. For example, in John 8:44, Jesus describes Satan as the father of lies who was a murderer from the start. Recognizing that lying, manipulation, and intimidation are his primary tools can help you start to see through his tactics. When you are aware of the enemy's methods, you gain the ability to confront them with truth rooted in the Word of God. You can take captive every thought that resists God's truth, standing on promises like Jeremiah 29:11, knowing that God's plan for your life is centered on hope and a future, regardless of what the enemy tries to whisper into your mind.

Distraction is one of the enemy's favorite weapons because it shifts your attention away from God's presence and promises. He might flood your mind with worries about your finances, relationships, or health, making it impossible to focus on what God has spoken over your life. In this state, faith weakens, and hope diminishes because your energy is consumed with the storm instead of the Savior. Recognizing when your thoughts are veering into distraction helps you to intentionally redirect your focus. Simple spiritual disciplines like prayer and meditating on scripture serve as anchors that bring your mind back to God's truth and away from the chaos that seeks to drown out His voice.

Lies are another core tactic used by the enemy to distort your perception of yourself, your circumstances, and God's character. These falsehoods often sound convincing because they are wrapped in partial truths or clichés that seem harmless on the surface. For example, he might whisper that your failure disqualifies you from God's love or that your pain indicates you are forsaken. Confronting these lies requires an active effort to replace them with God's Word. Memorizing scripture that affirms your identity in Christ, like Ephesians 1:4-5, allows you to counter the enemy's accusations with divine truth. Consistently declaring God's promises out loud has the power to break the hold of lies and reinforce your faith in God's faithfulness.

Intimidation manifests as fear, shame, and guilt designed to paralyze your spiritual progress. The enemy may threaten you with feelings of unworthiness or remind you of past mistakes that seem too shameful to overcome. He thrives on making you feel small and powerless, convincing you that you cannot stand or move forward. Recognizing this tactic invites you to boldly confront this fear with confidence rooted in Jesus' victory. Scriptures such as 2 Timothy 1:7 remind us that God's Spirit does not give us a spirit of fear but of power, love, and self-discipline. When you consciously choose to declare these truths, you push back against intimidation and regain your footing in Christ's strength. Regularly confessing God's sovereignty and your secure position in Him breaks the enemy's grip of fear and shame.

To strengthen your defense against these subtle tactics, develop a spiritual discipline that allows you to stay grounded in God's Word and prayer. Keep a journal of specific promises and truths from the Bible that speak to your situation. When feelings of distraction, lies, or intimidation arise, intentionally speak out these promises and declare your identity in Christ. Remember, the enemy only has as much power as you give him through ignorance or neglect of Scripture. By cultivating awareness and discernment, you build a spiritual armor that deflects his attacks before they take root. Small, consistent acts of faith and trust can gradually dismantle the enemy's tactics and restore your peace, hope, and purpose.

Identifying the Signs of Theft and Loss

When possessions or blessings are taken away unexpectedly, a disturbance often begins to stir deep within the soul. It's not just about losing material things; often, there is a spiritual heaviness that accompanies such loss. You may feel a sudden sense of emptiness, heaviness, or unease that didn't exist before. These feelings are more than just mood swings—they can be signals that something has been diverted from your life, whether through deception, spiritual warfare, or unseen forces working against your peace. Recognizing these signs requires spiritual sensitivity and honest reflection. For example, a sudden loss of joy, spiritual dryness, or a persistent sense of guilt or shame can be signs that an attack has been launched against your blessings. Sometimes, you might even feel as though your spiritual covering has been lifted, leaving you vulnerable and exposed. It's important to pay attention to these emotional and spiritual shifts because they often point toward a spiritual theft or attack. Scripture reminds us that the enemy comes to steal, kill, and destroy, but Jesus came to give us life abundantly. When our joy diminishes, our peace is disrupted, or our faith feels weak, it could indicate that something precious has been taken off course. Recognizing these indicators isn't about dwelling on the negativity but about awakening your discernment and waking up to the spiritual realities around you.

Accepting the reality of loss without harboring guilt or shame is a divine step toward healing and reclaiming what belongs to you. Loss can be a painful experience, especially when you believe you've done everything right, yet suddenly face hardship or setbacks. It's common to fall into a trap of guilt, questioning whether you failed God or missed something along the way. But scriptures clearly instruct us to cast our burdens on Him because He cares deeply for us. No guilt should linger when blessings or possessions are stolen because this is not a reflection of your worth or faithfulness. Instead, it serves as a reminder that we live in a fallen world, where spiritual warfare is real and attacks are part of the believer's journey. Accepting the loss means acknowledging it openly before God and refusing to let shame or blame dominate your heart. This is the foundation for moving forward with faith and purpose. Jesus Himself experienced loss—He was betrayed, rejected, and misunderstood—yet He remained steadfast in His mission. When you accept your pain honestly, you position yourself to reclaim your blessings confidently. Remember that Christ's victory on the cross assures us that nothing can truly be lost forever if we stay rooted in faith. Reclaiming what the enemy has stolen begins with faith, declaration, and a firm stand rooted in scripture."

To truly accept and process loss without guilt, speak the honest truth to God and remind yourself of His promises. Declare that you are not defined by what is gone but by what remains in Christ. Confess that you are a co-heir with Christ and that no weapon formed against you shall prosper. Use scriptures to reaffirm your identity: "The Lord will restore the years the locusts have eaten," and "you shall recover all." Creating a dedicated prayer time focused on reclaiming your blessings clears the spiritual air and activates heavenly provision. Keep your heart open for divine instructions, trusting that God will guide your steps toward spiritual and practical recovery. Use positive affirmations rooted in scripture to strengthen your faith during this season. Repetition of declarations like "My blessings are preserved in Christ," or "I refuse to accept spiritual theft," helps ground your thoughts in God's truth. Remember, the enemy thrives on confusion and guilt, but faith acts as a shield, reminding you that your blessings are not lost forever; they are in a process of restoration. Trusting God's sovereignty, you can stand firm, knowing that your divine inheritance is protected in Christ, and nothing can truly defeat what belongs to you in His kingdom.

What the Enemy Silenced, God Is Reviving

You've Been Quiet for Too Long

Not just silent, but **spiritually muted**.

There was a time you prayed bold prayers.

There was a time you sang until chains broke.

There was a time your words carried *weight*.

But then — betrayal, trauma, disappointment, warfare — and somewhere in that storm, your **voice was stolen**.

Not your literal voice, but your **spiritual authority**.

The enemy didn't just want your joy — he wanted your **vocal cords of faith**.

But God sent this word to you:

"Your voice is coming back. Your vow is being renewed. And your victory is non-negotiable."

GET BACK YOUR VOICE

Subheading: The Roar of the Redeemed

There's a **reason the enemy targeted your voice.** He knows that **your voice is a weapon.**

"The power of life and death is in the tongue…" – Proverbs 18:21

"Open your mouth wide, and I will fill it." – Psalm 81:10

The enemy silenced you because your **mouth births miracles**.

He wants you quiet because your declarations disturb his kingdom.

But hear this: **There is a sound assigned to your comeback.**

And it's time to **prophesy again.**

Real-Life Story: Dana's Silenced Prayers

Dana led worship in her church for years. When her marriage fell apart, she stopped singing. She stopped praying in front of others. Even her private prayers became whispers. She felt unworthy to lead.

Until one Sunday, while quietly sitting in the back, a visiting prophet stopped mid-sermon and pointed at her.

"God says — your voice is the key to your healing. Open your mouth and watch me restore you."

She broke in that moment, not in weakness, but in **worship**. Her cry returned. Her praise was raw. That week, she sang again — and not only did her heart heal, but so did others through her testimony.

GET BACK YOUR VOW

Realign with Your First Yes

Somewhere in the fight, **you forgot your first vow.**

Not to people, but to God.

- The **yes** you whispered as a child, when He first called you.
- The **yes** in that storm when you said, *"Lord, I'll serve You if You bring me through."*
- The **yes** before the delay, before the discouragement, before the detour.

But God never forgot it.

"When you make a vow to the Lord your God, you shall not delay to pay it… You must be careful to do what you've promised." – Deuteronomy 23:21-23

This isn't about work — it's about **returning to alignment.**

Some of the frustration you've felt isn't punishment — it's a **pull back to your original yes.**

Your Moment:

Take 60 seconds now and remember:

- What did you promise God before the storm hit?
  - What dream did you abandon?
 - What ministry did you put on the shelf?
 - What act of obedience have you delayed?

Say aloud: **"God, I'm ready to give you my yes again."**

GET BACK YOUR VICTORY

The Battle Is Already Won — Walk In It

You're not **fighting for victory** — you're fighting **for victory**.

"But thanks be to God! He gives us the victory through our Lord Jesus Christ." –

1 Corinthians 15:57

The enemy made you think your story ended in loss.

He made you forget that **you've already won**, because **He already won**.

Victory is not a feeling.

Victory is a **position**.

You may not see the full manifestation yet, but prophetically, it's done.

You're not trying to get back **to victory** — you're stepping back **into it**.

THE QUIET COMEBACK

Marlon had a prophetic call to preach — until addiction took over his life. He lost his family, his voice, and nearly his mind. For years, he wouldn't step into a church. But one day, at a recovery meeting, someone asked him to pray.

He did — with a shaking voice and tears. But something **ignited**.

Three years later, Marlon preaches in prisons, rehab centers, and online to thousands. He says:

"The enemy tried to bury my voice in shame. But God gave me victory wrapped in grace."

ACTIVATIONS

. DECREE TO TAKE BACK YOUR VOICE:

"My voice carries heaven's authority.

I will speak, sing, pray, preach, and praise with boldness.

The enemy will no longer mute me. I will not stay quiet in the presence of chaos.

I have a sound, and I'm releasing it."

RECOMMIT YOUR VOW TO GOD:

Write it in your journal or speak it aloud:

"Lord, I return to my vow. I say YES again. I give you my will, my voice, my assignment. I pick up what I put down. I forgive those who discouraged me. I'm back — and I'm ready."

YOU'RE NOT POWERLESS — YOU'RE POSITIONED

You didn't lose your voice forever.

You didn't break your vow for good.

You didn't forfeit your victory.

God is **restoring everything**.

"The Lord will fight for you; you need only to be still." – Exodus 14:14

"Behold, I give you authority… over all the power of the enemy." – Luke 10:19

"You will also decree a thing, and it will be established for you." – Job 22:28

This is your divine moment.

Speak again.

Say yes again.

Win again.

What the enemy took, Heaven is giving back with power —
and it starts with your voice.

UNDERSTANDING THE SPIRIT OF DECEPTION

Deception often works quietly, carving out lies that seem believable enough to distort your perception of who God truly is and what His word declares. It can operate subtly, whispering false narratives into your mind, telling you that God's promises aren't for you, or that your pain and struggles mean He has abandoned you. Over time, these lies can cloud your understanding, making it difficult to see God's truth clearly. When brokenness and setbacks happen, deception tends to magnify doubt, cast shadows on your faith, and convince you that healing or restoration isn't possible. It's like looking through a foggy lens that distorts reality, preventing you from perceiving God's love and promises as they truly are.

Deception often thrives in vulnerability. When we're hurting, confused, or exhausted from life's battles, we become easier targets for lies to take root. It may come through feelings of guilt, shame, or condemnation, convincing us that our circumstances reflect God's displeasure or disfavor. Sometimes, it manifests as the voice of fear whispering that our past mistakes have disqualified us from God's grace, or that our faith isn't enough to see us through. These lies distort the truth by filtering reality through a lens of defeat rather than victory. The enemy capitalizes on our pain, using it to foster doubt about God's goodness, His faithfulness, and His willingness to heal and restore. Recognizing these distortions is the first step toward breaking free from deception's grip.

Deception also shifts focus away from God's promises to our problems. It can make believers fixate on their circumstances rather than on God's power to change them. For example, rather than proclaiming that God is able to turn mourning into dancing, deception may cause someone to believe that their loss is permanent, that healing isn't on the horizon. It traps individuals in a cycle of negative thinking and spiritual paralysis. The more a person listens to lies, such as "You'll never recover," "God doesn't care," or "Your faith has failed," the more their perception becomes skewed and their recovery is delayed. These distortions hinder not just understanding but also practical steps forward, leading many to accept defeat instead of standing on God's truth as their foundation.

Deception often masquerades as truth because it preys on what seems familiar or comforting. It may use Scripture taken out of context or twisted to fit a lie, fooling even the most sincere believers. For instance, someone might be convinced that their suffering is a punishment from God rather than a test or a redemptive process. This misinterpretation distorts biblical truth and can discourage faith and perseverance. Spiritual deception is more than ignorance; it's a strategy that feeds on our weaknesses and exploits our emotional wounds. To see through it, believers need to develop spiritual discernment, which comes from knowing God's Word deeply and allowing the Holy Spirit to expose lies that any enemy of our soul tries to plant. Without this discernment, deception can become a barrier that blocks the path to healing and clarity.

Fighting deception begins with anchoring your heart and mind in God's Word—the ultimate truth that pierces through every lie. Scriptures like John 8:32 remind us that "the truth will set you free," signaling that God's Word holds the power to unveil lies and restore our perspective. When deceptive thoughts arise, declaring and meditating on His promises shifts our focus from despair to hope. For example, reminding yourself that God's mercy is new every morning (Lamentations 3:22-23) helps combat feelings of guilt or unworthiness. Biblical truths act as spiritual anchors, providing clarity amid confusion and helping shift your perception from what the enemy whispers to what God has spoken.

Developing a strong foundation on Scripture also means understanding its context and applying it confidently. Studying the Word diligently and meditating on key promises—such as Romans 8:37, which declares that we are more than conquerors through Christ—empowers believers to oppose lies with truth. Prayer is another vital tool; asking the Holy Spirit to reveal deception and illuminate God's truth within your heart ensures you are not battling spiritual lies on your own. When doubts come, citation of these truths acts as spiritual weapons protecting your mind and your faith. Over time, consistently standing on God's promises will establish a new mindset rooted in victory rather than defeat. It's about replacing the enemy's lies with God's eternal truth—the truth that sets the captives free.

Another way to stay grounded is through community and accountability. Engaging with mature believers who can speak truth into your life creates a shield against deception. Sometimes, we're too close to the pain to see clearly, and others can help identify when lies are taking hold. Celebrate the testimonies of those who have overcome similar struggles—they serve as living proof that God's truth prevails. Remember that spiritual warfare involves not just defensive stands but also active declarations of God's promises. Recognize that victory flows from knowing the Word, speaking it boldly, and trusting the Holy Spirit to guide your understanding. As you keep your focus on God's truth, the fog of deception begins to lift, revealing the clarity of His purpose and victory in your life.

Finally, stay alert to how deception may come disguised as comfort or advice. Always compare what you hear with Scripture and seek God's wisdom in prayer. In doing so, you position yourself to recognize and reject lies promptly, preventing them from taking deep root. Remember, the enemy's aim is to keep you bound and blind to God's truth, but Jesus came to set the captives free—so hold onto His Word, and refuse to accept anything that contradicts His promises. A simple but powerful step is to declare God's Word aloud in moments of doubt—affirming truth over lie—until your mind is flooded with faith and hope again. Keeping God's Word close in your heart becomes your strongest defense against deception's subtle attacks.

BIBLICAL FOUNDATIONS OF RESTORATION

Figure 2.1

God's Promises to Restore What Was Taken

Throughout scripture, God makes clear His unwavering commitment to restore what the enemy has stolen from His people. These promises aren't just poetic words; they are declarations of divine intent rooted in His nature. When looking at the Word, you find numerous verses affirming that God's heart is to bring back and restore everything lost, whether it be time, joy, peace, or even relationships. For example, Psalm 126:5-6 speaks of those who sow with tears, promising they will reap with songs of joy. This isn't just poetic language; it's a divine guarantee that God works through seasons of loss to bring about restoration in greater measure. The promises declare that no matter how deep the loss, God's intention remains to heal, rebuild, and restore. These scriptures serve as anchors for faith during times when everything seems broken, reaffirming that restoration is part of God's plan for His children.

Several scriptural promises stand out as steadfast declarations of God's heart to restore. Joel 2:25 is one such verse, where God reassures His people that He will restore the years the locust has eaten. This passage emphasizes that God not only restores what was lost but exceeds it by bringing a harvest far greater than before. It's a powerful reminder that God can revive even the most decayed circumstances, turning tragedy into testimony. Similarly, Psalm 23:3 reveals God's role as a shepherd who restores the soul.

This verse offers comfort, highlighting that God actively works to revive spirits that are drained and broken. These promises remind believers that God's restoration is comprehensive, covering emotional wounds, lost blessings, and hope for the future. Believing in these divine assurances positions us to expect restoration, even when the journey seems long or difficult.

Walking in faith means holding fast to these divine words, allowing them to shape our perspective on loss and healing. The beauty of God's promises is that they are not empty claims but rooted in His unwavering character. Hebrews 10:23 encourages us to hold tightly to the hope we profess, for He who promised is faithful. When doubt crests our hearts, declaring these promises over our lives can reinforce our resolve to trust that God's goodness will prevail. It's also helpful to remember that God's promises often come with specific conditions—faith, prayer, repentance, and perseverance. When approaching these truths, it's essential to align our hearts with God's Word, trusting that His promises will manifest during the right season. Whether it's reclaiming lost relationships, restoring health, or renewing joy, these scriptures serve as divine anchors that keep us grounded in hope. By memorizing and meditating on these promises, we build a firm foundation on which faith can stand firm, confidently awaiting the fulfillment of God's restoration plans.

Faith Anchors in Times of Loss

In times of loss or setbacks, the foundation of your faith must be rooted deeply in God's Word. When hurt and disappointment threaten to shake your confidence, the promises found in Scripture serve as anchors that hold you steady. The Bible is full of declarations of God's unchanging character—His faithfulness, love, and sovereignty—that remain true regardless of life's circumstances. To build unwavering faith, immerse yourself daily in these promises, letting them inscribe hope deep into your heart. Remember, faith is not a fleeting emotion but a steadfast trust rooted in knowing who God is and what He has spoken. Repeating scriptures aloud, meditating on His promises, and allowing His Word to shape your perspective form a resilient shield against doubt. When disappointment arises, recall the truths you have stored in your heart and declare them over your circumstances. This practice trains your mind and spirit to lean on God's Word as your primary source of strength, encouraging you to stand firm even when everything around you seems uncertain or broken. Faith grounded in God's Word becomes a weapon that dispels despair and affirms that God's plans for you are still unfolding beyond your current pain.

Prayer is more than a routine; it is a direct line of communication with the Father, inviting His presence into your brokenness. When disappointment presses in, prayer becomes a personal refuge—a place to pour out your frustrations, receive divine comfort, and align your heart with God's purposes. Meditation on Scripture complements prayer by helping you dwell on God's truths, making them a part of your inner conversation. Scripture meditation involves slowly contemplating verses that speak to God's promises, His love, and His unwavering support. Sit quietly, read a verse, and reflect on how it applies to your life, allowing it to renew your mind and recalibrate your emotions. This intentional focus on God's Word can guard your heart against discouragement and redirect your thoughts toward hope. Over time, these spiritual disciplines become an anchor that stabilizes your soul, keeps hope burning brightly, and reminds you that God's faithfulness endures even in the hardest seasons.

Practically, set aside specific times each day to engage in Scripture reading and prayer, making it a non-negotiable part of your routine. As you do so, begin each session with a genuine prayer asking the Holy Spirit to open your eyes to God's truths and to strengthen your faith. Choose key scriptures that speak directly to your situation—verses that affirm God's sovereignty, His love, and His promises to restore and uplift. Write these verses down and keep them in places where you'll see them often: on your mirror, in your wallet, or as a screensaver. Speak them aloud frequently, especially during moments of doubt or emotional pain. Over time, this consistent focus will help rewire your thought patterns, replacing despair with hope rooted in God's Word. Remember, faith is built step-by-step through a daily commitment to God's promises and a persistent pursuit of His presence. By anchoring your soul in Scripture and prayer, you create an unshakable foundation that can uphold you through any storm of loss or disappointment.

Jesus' Example of Recovery and Victory

Jesus' experience of rising from the dead is the ultimate symbol of victory over impossible circumstances. His journey wasn't just about conquering physical death; it was about revealing that even the darkest moments can give way to new beginnings. When we consider His suffering, His betrayal, and His crucifixion, we see a path of intense hardship, yet also a divine purpose that led to resurrection and restored life. This story serves as a powerful blueprint for anyone facing setbacks or loss, reminding us that defeat isn't the end but a step towards divine restoration. His example teaches us that recovery begins with belief—faith in God's power to turn mourning into dancing, death into life, brokenness into wholeness. If Jesus overcame death, then whatever challenges you face, no matter how insurmountable they seem, can be transformed through His victorious power.

Reflecting on His journey invites us to see ourselves in His story. Just as Jesus endured betrayal, rejection, and suffering, we too face times of hardship, loss, and brokenness. Yet, Jesus's resurrection proves that these moments are not the final chapter. His victory over death is a blueprint showing us that setbacks are temporary and that God's purpose remains intact even in our darkest seasons.

When you meditate on His journey, you begin to understand that recovery is rooted in faith, trusting that God's plan includes a triumphant ending. His resurrection is not just about conquering death, but about restoring life, purpose, and hope to those who believe in Him. Use this story as a source of strength when discouragement tries to creep in, remembering that God's power to restore is greater than any loss or pain.

Christ's victory did not end with His resurrection; it marked the beginning of an authority given to His followers—the power to reclaim and restore what the enemy has stolen. Throughout His earthly ministry, Jesus demonstrated authority over sickness, nature, and spiritual darkness. After His resurrection, He declared that His disciples would also walk in this same authority, empowering them to stand against defeat and reclaim their inheritance. For those recovering from loss or setbacks, embracing this authority means declaring over your life that you are not powerless; God's victorious power resides within you. You are called to rise up with confidence, speaking life and blessing into your circumstances, knowing that Jesus has already secured your victory. This authority isn't just for spiritual battles but extends to every area of life where you have experienced theft—whether it's health, relationships, or dreams—because Jesus's victory is complete and all-encompassing.

To truly walk in this authority, it begins with a firm belief that what Jesus accomplished on the cross is also for you. You must speak victory over your situation, declaring that every stolen piece of your life will be restored. Sometimes, it involves actively rebuking the enemy's attempts to keep you in a place of despair or defeat. Remember, Christ's resurrection power equips you to boldly declare God's promises and to stand firm in faith. Reclaim what has been taken by praying with authority, declaring God's Word out loud, and refusing to accept defeat as final. Walking in this victorious authority transforms how you approach setbacks—no longer as signs of failure but as opportunities to see God's power at work restoring and bringing forth new life. Your words, backed by faith, become instruments of reclamation, turning every loss into a testimony of God's grace.

Know that your recovery is a spiritual act of reclaiming what was once yours by divine right. Jesus's victory empowers you to step into a new level of faith, where you believe that God's promises are yes and amen. Stand firm and declare that you are more than a conqueror through Christ, and that every area of your life that the enemy has tried to ravage will be restored with abundance. As you do, you align yourself with the victorious authority Christ has given you, releasing divine power to reclaim and rebuild your life. This is not just about hoping for the best but actively exercising your spiritual authority, trusting that God's power is working behind the scenes to bring full restoration. Remember, the resurrection power lives in you, making you more than capable of walking out your victory today and every day afterward.

3// CONFRONTING PAIN AND DISAPPOINTMENT

Figure 3.1

Honoring Your Feelings with Integrity

Opening your heart before God to acknowledge your pain may feel vulnerable at first, but it is a crucial step toward genuine healing. When you bring your honest feelings before the Lord, without hiding or numbing them, you create space for divine comfort and restoration to enter. Guilt can often tempt us to minimize or suppress our hurt, but scripturally, God invites us to come as we are—broken, confused, hurting—so that His grace can meet us there. By being truthful with Him, you affirm that your feelings are valid and that your pain matters in His presence. This openness doesn't mean you're weak; rather, it demonstrates a deep trust in God's ability to handle our rawest emotions, opening the door for His healing power to flow into every wounded part.

Understanding that expressing hurt is not a sign of weakness but a vital step toward a breakthrough is transformative. When we hide our pain or pretend we're okay, we often prolong the damage and delay the healing process. Emotions like anger, disappointment, or grief are signals pointing us to areas where we need God's intervention. By listening to these signals and allowing ourselves to feel deeply, we not only release pent-up feelings but also activate a path toward restoration. Sharing our hurt with trusted individuals or journaling our emotions are practical ways to process what we are experiencing. Remember, in scripture, many biblical figures openly expressed their pain—David lamented, Job cried out, and Jesus Himself poured out His anguish in Gethsemane. Their honesty paved the way for divine encounters that brought new hope and strength, illustrating that vulnerability is a bridge to wholeness.

Honoring feelings with integrity involves speaking truthfully about what you're enduring while anchoring your honesty in faith. This means acknowledging your pain without shame and maintaining a posture of humility before God, trusting that He is always present and able to heal. Be aware, though, that this process may stir up uncomfortable memories or emotions; giving yourself grace during these moments is essential. It's helpful to create a safe environment where your feelings can be expressed freely—whether through prayer, worship, or trusted fellowship. As you grow in honesty with God, you begin to see your pain not as a failure or a flaw, but as a part of your human story that God is actively redeeming. Let your transparency become a declaration of faith that even brokenness can lead to a deeper understanding of His love and grace.

And remember, the act of being truthful about your hurt is not a one-time event but an ongoing journey. Regularly checking in with God about your emotional state keeps you connected to His peace amid chaos. Practice speaking openly to Him, saying honestly what's in your heart, even when it feels difficult. Over time, you may find that the weight of unspoken pain lifts, replaced by a renewed sense of trust and hope. This honest dialogue shifts your perspective from seeing pain as a sign of failure to recognizing it as a pathway to deeper intimacy with God. When you honor your feelings with integrity, you create space for divine healing that transforms your brokenness into a testimony of His grace, making room for renewal even in the deepest wounds. Keep in mind that your emotional honesty can also inspire others around you to trust God more fully with their own hurts.

Choosing Forgiveness Over Offense

Forgiveness is not merely an act; it is a divine release that sets your heart free from the chains of bitterness and pain. When you choose to forgive, you are not excusing what was done or denying the hurt; instead, you are surrendering the power that offense has over you. Resentment can quietly take root, festering beneath the surface and impacting your emotional well-being, relationships, and spiritual health. Choosing forgiveness breaks that grip and allows your heart to heal and move forward with peace. It is a conscious decision to let go of the need for revenge or justice in your own strength and to trust God's justice and mercy to handle the rest.

True forgiveness requires an intentional shift in perspective. It often starts with acknowledging the pain, but then translating that pain into a prayer of release. Jesus's words on the cross, "Father, forgive them, for they know not what they do," serve as a powerful example. Forgiveness is a divine act that aligns us with God's heart and His commands. When we forgive, we are not denying the damage done; rather, we are releasing ourselves from the bondage of holding onto hurt, which only prolongs our suffering. Forgiveness doesn't erase the past, but it frees us from living as prisoners to it. This act of surrender is a declaration that our peace is more valuable than our pain.

Holding onto resentment can act as a barrier to God's blessings in our lives. It's like carrying a heavy weight that exhausts, distracts, and stifles us. But forgiveness lifts that burden, opening the door for healing—emotionally, spiritually, and physically. Whenever resentment attempts to reassert itself, reminding yourself of Christ's example of forgiveness—the ultimate act of love and mercy—can strengthen your resolve. Remember, forgiveness is a process, not a one-time event. It might involve repeated prayers, renewed declarations of faith, and choosing to respond differently each time hurt resurfaces. Faith becomes the foundation that sustains your decision to forgive, as you trust God to restore and heal your broken places. Your acts of forgiveness serve as a testament to His power working within you, breaking cycles of pain and ushering in divine peace.

Choosing to forgive others is more than an act of kindness; it is a pathway to spiritual freedom and divine restoration. Many women have faced betrayal, disappointment, or rejection, which often leave scars that threaten their peace and faith. Forgiveness, however, unlocks the door to spiritual release. When you forgive, you are aligning yourself with God's divine nature, which is merciful and forgiving. This act is not just about restoring relationships; it's about restoring your soul and reconnecting with God's purpose for your life. Forgiving others also clears the way for divine blessings to flow freely into your life, unblocked by the weight of unforgiveness.

Understanding that forgiveness is a choice gives you the power to take back control over your emotions and spiritual health. It's about deciding to release offenses, no matter how deeply rooted they may be. Forgiveness allows divine restoration to occur as it transforms bitterness into mercy, hatred into love, and pain into peace. Many women have discovered that forgiving someone releases not only the offender but also frees them from the prison of ongoing hurt. It's important to remember that God's forgiveness of us is the template—He forgives freely and completely. When we choose to forgive others, we mirror God's mercy and open ourselves to receive His divine restoration. This act of obedience not only heals wounds but also restores hope and faith in God's goodness and sovereignty.

Practically, learning to forgive involves several steps: recognizing the offense, choosing to forgive, praying for the offender, and releasing the hurt to God. It may also require ongoing prayer and affirmation, especially when old feelings resurface. Trusting God to handle justice and to heal wounds is central to forgiving authentically. It's often in the act of forgiving that divine restoration takes place—not only in broken relationships but also within our own hearts. Displaying forgiveness demonstrates spiritual maturity and aligns us with God's divine purpose for our lives. As we forgive, we make room for divine blessings, joy, and peace to flow into our hearts and to be a testimony of His transforming power in our lives.

One practical tip to foster forgiveness is to declare daily that you choose to forgive and to ask God for the strength to do so. Retrieving biblical promises and scriptures about mercy and forgiveness, then meditating on them regularly, can keep your heart aligned with God's will. Remember, forgiving others isn't just about them—it's a divine act that leads to your spiritual health and divine restoration. The more you lean on God's grace, the easier it becomes to release offenses and receive His healing. Forgiveness is often the missing link in healing, growth, and divine breakthrough. When the Spirit prompts you to forgive, step out in faith—trust that God's power is flowing through your act of obedience, paving the way for healing and divine restoration to unfold in your life.

Healing Through God's Comfort

When life feels heavy and your heart is overwhelmed, trusting in God's presence becomes the anchor that holds you steady. It's in these dark moments that faith is truly tested, yet it is also where God reveals His deep compassion. Remember that God is always near; His promise in Psalm 34:18 affirms, The Lord is close to the brokenhearted and saves those who are crushed in spirit. Even if you can't see Him or feel His presence, trusting that He is with you creates space for healing. This trust is not about denying your pain but choosing to believe that God's presence surrounds you at all times, especially when nothing else seems to make sense.

Holding onto this truth allows you to shift your focus from the storm around you to the One who calms it within you. That's a key step—learning to lean into the assurance that God's presence is more real than your circumstances. During moments of despair, whisper to Him with honesty, sharing your pain and doubts, knowing He is listening. As you do, you open your heart to experience His peace — a peace that surpasses understanding — and it begins to anchor you securely in His love. Real trust isn't silent belief but a conscious choice to walk with Him, especially when every step feels uncertain. This act of trusting transforms moments of pain into opportunities for divine encounter, reminding you that you're never alone, no matter how silent the night may seem.

Developing this trust is a practice rooted in scripture and reinforced through personal encounters. You may find it helpful to set aside intentional times to remind yourself of His promises and meditate on His Word. Scriptures like Isaiah 41:10 offer powerful reassurance: So do not fear, for I am with you. Repeating these truths aloud can renew your mind and bolster your confidence that God's presence is your refuge. As your trust deepens, every dark moment becomes an invitation to experience a greater depth of His comfort, unfolding His love in ways that words can't fully express. Trusting His presence transforms your perspective from despair to hope, reminding you that no darkness can extinguish His light shining within you.

God's healing balm is more than mere comfort; it is an active, restorative power that reaches into the deepest wounds of your spirit. When pain or grief has left scars on your soul, it can feel impossible to heal on your own. Yet, the scripture assures us that the Lord is the Healer—He alone can mend what is broken and restore what is lost. Psalm 147:3 declares, "He heals the brokenhearted and binds up their wounds." Receiving His healing begins with surrender—acknowledging your need for His touch and trusting that His balm is available. As you do, you invite divine healing into every vulnerable place within you, allowing His soothing presence to work where your human efforts often fall short.

There are particular ways to permit this divine balm to work effectively. First, intentionally bring your wounds before Him in prayer, sharing honestly what hurts and what you don't understand.

Then, choose to believe that His grace is sufficient to cover all pain, no matter how deep. As His healing flows into your heart, you'll notice a gradual change—an easing of burdens, a lifting of discouragement, a renewal of strength. This process isn't always quick, but it is consistent when you stay grounded in faith. Sometimes, it's helpful to visualize His healing balm as a gentle, warm oil poured over your wounds, penetrating into the pain and bringing relief. Over time, you find that your spirit begins to regain vitality, hope blooms anew, and strength rises as you firmly trust in His restorative power.

Remember, renewal often comes layer by layer. What seems impossible today can become a powerful testimony tomorrow of God's ability to heal and restore. Keep leaning into His promises, knowing that the healing journey is a testament to His unfailing love. As His balm continues to soothe your wounded spirit, you'll discover fresh courage and renewed strength to face whatever lies ahead. The key is to trust Him completely, refusing to carry your burdens alone, and instead placing them into His capable hands, opening your heart fully for His healing touch. Through this process, the Lord will renew your strength in ways that cause you to stand tall again, healthier and more vibrant, ready to carry His light into the world around you.

4// DECREE AND DECLARATION: RECLAIMING WHAT IS RIGHTFULLY YOURS

Figure 4.1

The Power of Spoken Faith

Faith is not just a feeling; it is a spoken word that holds active power. When you declare God's promises aloud, you send a powerful signal to the spiritual realm that you believe in His ability to restore, heal, and restore what the enemy has stolen. It starts with understanding that God's Word is alive and sharper than any two-edged sword. By speaking scriptures like Joel 2:25, which promises the restoration of everything the locusts have eaten, you are aligning your words with divine truth. These declarations are not mere words; they are spiritual weapons that carve a path through darkness and doubt. Every time you speak the promises of God over your situation, you reinforce your faith and create an atmosphere ripe for divine intervention.

However, it's important that these declarations come from a sincere heart, rooted in belief and not just repetition. When you proclaim God's Word, do so with conviction, knowing that His Word does not return void. Your voice, combined with faith, sets in motion the restoration process. For example, declaring, The Lord restores my soul and everything stolen from me, grounded in Psalm 23:3, becomes an oath of faith. Personalize scripture to fit your circumstances, or speak aloud the promises that have spoken to your spirit during your quiet moments with God. This act of speaking is a vital step in reclaiming what has been lost—be it health, relationships, or hope. It's a declaration of trust in a God who can bring dead things back to life and turn mourning into dancing.

Creating a daily routine of bold declarations can be a game-changer in your recovery process. Write out scriptures that speak specifically to your needs—whether it's healing, financial provision, or emotional restoration. Then, recite these words aloud each day, preferably in the morning as a fresh declaration of faith. As you speak these promises, visualize them coming to pass, and thank God in advance for His work. Remember, your words carry power, and consistent confession signals to heaven that you are serious about your faith. Over time, these declarations will transform your perspective, fortify your spirit, and position you for divine breakthroughs. Trust that when you speak God's Word, heaven responds, and your circumstances begin to shift according to divine timing and purpose.

Understanding that your words carry authority is crucial when engaging in spiritual warfare. In the spiritual realm, words are not passive; they are active agents that can either empower or weaken your position. Jesus Himself demonstrated this power when He rebuked demons and commanded situations to change through spoken words. Matthew 8:16 tells us that Jesus cast out spirits with a simple command, showing the authority believers possess when aligned with God's Word. As children of God, you are called to speak with confidence, knowing that your declarations are backed by heaven's authority. This authority is not rooted in your own strength, but in Christ who lives within you. When you declare God's promises over your life, you are effectively wielding spiritual weapons that can dismantle the enemy's assignments and reclaim what was taken.

Spiritual warfare involves actively resisting the enemy's tactics through the power of your words. It's about recognizing that the enemy seeks to steal, kill, and destroy—yet Christ came to give life more abundantly. You are empowered to stand firm against ambitions of despair, sickness, or defeat by speaking God's truth. For example, declaring, in Jesus' name, I break every assignment of the enemy over my finances and declare divine provision, aligns your words with spiritual authority. It's important to understand that in this warfare, your words are not just wishful thinking but strategic declarations rooted in biblical authority. When pressed with doubts or fear, remind yourself of your spiritual identity and your position as a victor through Christ. Your words are the divine keys that unlock heaven's resources, bring down strongholds, and set the captives free.

This authority is also about understanding divine recovery. God desires for His children to recover every lost blessing, every piece of brokenness, and every moment of sorrow. As heirs and joint heirs with Christ, you have access to the throne of grace where divine power flows. Using your voice to proclaim recovery according to scripture is an act of claiming your inheritance. For example, in Joel 2:32, God declares that everyone who calls on His name shall be saved and rescued. This promise isn't limited to salvation; it extends to every area in which you need divine intervention. Recognizing your authority to declare victory and divine recovery shifts your mindset from victim to victor. It's through these declarations that heaven's gates open, releasing God's power to bring restoration and restitution into your life.

Scriptural Declarations for Recovery

Declaring God's promises aloud can become a powerful act of faith that shifts your perspective from doubt to trust. When you speak scripture over your life, it's like releasing God's truth into your circumstances, making His word your personal decree. Instead of focusing on what you've lost or what setbacks you've faced, these confessions help reframe your mind to see God's intent for abundance, restoration, and victory. Each declaration reinforces the truth that God's promises are real and accessible, especially when you declare them in faith. Make it a habit to choose specific scriptures that speak directly to your situation—whether it's provision, healing, or emotional recovery—and speak them boldly, with conviction, as if you already possess what God's word affirms.

For instance, you can declare, The Lord is my shepherd; I shall not want (Psalm 23:1) over your finances or possessions, or "The Lord will restore what the enemy has stolen from me" (Joel 2:25). These declarations create a spiritual atmosphere where faith begins to take root and grow stronger. It's important that these confessions come from your heart, not just your lips, so take time meditating on the truth behind each scripture. When you align your words with God's promises, you position yourself under His authority, inviting divine intervention and favor. Over time, these declarations become a shield against discouragement, reminding you that God's word is active, living, and able to accomplish what it says.

Remember, the goal is to make these confessions a daily habit, turning your mouth into a tool for speaking life and victory. As you form this practice, you'll start noticing a shift in your faith—confidence rising, doubt diminishing, and your focus returning to God's power to restore and reconcile. According to biblical principles, speaking His word aloud is not just about reciting scriptures but about aligning your heart to God's promises. These declarations have the potential to unleash spiritual forces that fight for your breakthroughs, creating an environment where God's promises can manifest visibly in your life and possessions. Keep in mind that consistency is key—faith builds as you repeatedly declare God's promises with unwavering trust.

Repetition of scriptural declarations is more than just saying words over and over; it's about planting powerful truths deep into your spirit. When you say these words daily, they begin to transform your mindset from one of scarcity or defeat to one of abundance and victory. It's like watering a seed—each affirmation nourishes your faith, strengthening your confidence that God is faithful to perform what He has promised. Daily declarations act as spiritual armor, protecting your mind from negative thoughts and doubt that try to undermine your recovery. As you make these confessions part of your regular routine—whether morning, evening, or anytime during the day—they become a foundation for building hope, perseverance, and victory.

Consistency in repeating these declarations also creates a habit of faith that overrides the noise of discouragement and defeat. When setbacks seem overwhelming, speaking God's promises over your life reminds you that your circumstances are not the final word. Instead, His word is the truth that molds your reality. Some find it helpful to write their favorite declarations on sticky notes or in a prayer journal, making it easier to remind themselves during busy moments. As you persist in daily reinforcement, you'll notice a shift in your attitude and spiritual posture—more peaceful, confident, and aware of God's ability to bring restoration. Eventually, these words become part of your inner dialogue, shaping your thoughts and actions toward faith-based victory. Remember, the more you declare, the more your faith is stirred to see God's promise fulfilled in your life and possessions.

Another practical tip is to tailor your declarations to your specific needs and situation. Personalize scriptures so they resonate deeply within your heart, making your confessions more authentic and powerful. For example, if your goal is financial recovery, declare, God supplies all my needs according to His riches in glory (Philippians 4:19). If emotional healing is your focus, say, The Lord will comfort those who mourn and turn their mourning into joy (Isaiah 61:3). As you develop this practice, you actively participate in a spiritual warfare that aligns your words with God's divine plan. Keep your declarations simple, rooted in scripture, and spoken with authority—as if you are already living in the fullness of what God has promised. Over time, these repeated truths will build your faith and keep your hope alive, helping you walk in victory regardless of current circumstances.

Creating Your Personal Warfare Script

Building a warfare script rooted in Scripture begins with a clear understanding of your identity in Christ and the authority that comes with it. Start by reflecting on the promises of God's Word that affirm His power and your place as a conqueror through Jesus. Select declarations that resonate deeply within your heart, affirming God's truth over your life and circumstances. For example, verses like 2 Corinthians 10:4-5 emphasize the divine power to demolish strongholds, giving you a foundation to declare victory over fear, doubt, and spiritual oppression. Personalize each declaration so that it feels authentic, spoken with conviction and belief, as if God Himself is affirming your authority. Writing out these declarations brings clarity and focus, transforming vague hopes into powerful, specific affirmations that you can declare with certainty at any moment.

Using your script in prayer and worship solidifies your spiritual authority and serves as a weapon against every form of attack. When you speak these declarations aloud, you activate the spiritual realm, confronting the enemy head-on with God's truth. It's not just about reciting words; it's about declaring with authority, as if you're asserting a divine legal right over your life. Incorporate your declarations into your daily prayer time, standing firm in faith as you remind yourself of your position in Christ. Worship becomes a battlefield where your voice rises in praise and declaration, dismantling the lies and replacing them with God's promises. Through consistent use, your script transforms from mere words into a spiritual sword that cuts through despair, breaking the chains of deception and reclaiming what belongs to you, whether it's peace, health, provision, or emotional healing.

To make your warfare script truly effective, approach it with a sense of boldness and transparency. Share personal stories of previous victories, testifying to God's faithfulness. Remember, your words carry power because they are spoken in faith and backed by Scripture. As you declare God's Word over your life, expect breakthroughs. Keep your declarations simple but full of authority—statements like "I am more than a conqueror in Christ," or "The Lord fights for me; I will hold my peace." Repeat these regularly, especially during moments of struggle or spiritual drought. The more you declare, the more you reinforce your identity in Christ and weaken the enemy's foothold. Over time, you'll see your faith sharpened and your spiritual momentum increase, helping you stand firm even amidst the fiercest battles.

5// THE STRATEGIES OF SPIRITUAL WARFARE

Binding and Loosing in the Spirit

Understanding how to bind and loose is foundational to walking in spiritual authority and seeing God's power manifest in our lives. When we talk about binding, we are essentially tying up or restricting the influence of darkness—whether it be fear, sickness, debt, or deception—by commanding it to leave. Losing, on the other hand, involves releasing the blessings, promises, and divine breakthroughs that God has prepared for us. This process isn't just about wishful thinking; it's about aligning our tongues and actions with God's Word, speaking what He says about our circumstances, and taking authority in prayer. The power to do this comes from Jesus Christ, who has given believers authority over all the power of the enemy (Luke 10:19). As we learn to exercise that authority, we become active participants in what the Spirit is doing in the spiritual realm, opening doors for blessings and closing doors to enemy attacks. Engaging in this warfare requires faith, unwavering belief in God's Word, and a deliberate decision to resist every form of defeat or opposition. It invites us to examine the words we speak daily—because death and life are in the power of the tongue—and choose to declare what God's promises say, rather than what the enemy tries to impose. In practice, binding and loosing involve prayer, declarations, and spiritual authority exercised consistently, creating a spiritual environment where God's will can flourish and darkness is pushed back.

Operating in spiritual authority to release God's power over your circumstances is not just a lofty concept for spiritual giants but a truth available to every believer. Jesus' role as our Lord and Savior restored our position of authority that was lost in the fall. When we understand that we are seated with Him in heavenly places (Ephesians 2:6), it becomes clearer that our words carry power. Speaking God's truth over our situations and using our authority to command the enemy to depart sets the stage for divine interventions. It begins with recognizing God's promises in Scripture—promises of healing, provision, victory, and peace—and boldly declaring them over our lives. For example, if there's a financial crisis, declaring Scriptures like Philippians 4:19—My God shall supply all my needs—coupled with prayer and faith, can open a spiritual door for provision. Operating in authority also means standing firm when challenges come, refusing to accept defeat as final, and consistently declaring God's truth until manifestations appear. This is not about empty words but about speaking in alignment with Heaven, backed by faith and confidence that God's power is at work. When you exercise this authority, you shift not only your circumstances but also influence spiritual atmospheres around you, breaking cycles of hardship and releasing divine favor into your life.

Practically, operating in spiritual authority involves several key steps that believers can implement daily. First, start with prayer—praying aloud and declaring God's Word over your specific situation. Second, identify the enemy's schemes by discerning what lies or attacks are targeting you—whether it's fear, addiction, sickness, or discouragement—and confront them with Scripture and authority. Third, use authoritative declarations, speaking God's promises as if they are already fulfilled. For example, "I am healed by Jesus' stripes," or "God's peace rules in my mind and my home." Fourth, maintain consistency—don't just pray once and forget; continue to declare and stand in faith, knowing that spiritual battles are often won through persistent and unwavering faith. Build a habit of confessing victory over your circumstances, knowing that your words carry divine power. Remember, the enemy's goal is to keep you defeated and silent, but your response with spiritual authority releases divine power that shifts the spiritual atmosphere, positioning you for breakthrough. Staying grounded in God's Word and exercising consistent authority in faith shifts the spiritual environment, creating room for God's promises to manifest visibly in your life.

Utilizing Prayer as a Weapon

In spiritual warfare, prayer is not just a routine act; it is a powerful weapon designed to confront darkness and bring light. When you recognize that deception often operates in hidden places, praying with intent and focus becomes essential. Fervency in prayer means pouring your heart out with sincerity and passion, fully believing that heaven responds to genuine cries. Targeted prayer involves addressing specific issues—refusing to settle for vague requests—asking God to reveal the hidden schemes of the enemy, and dismantle them. This kind of prayer awakens your spiritual senses, allowing you to see beyond the surface and confront spiritual deception head-on.

Scripture anchors this approach vividly. Jesus urged his followers to watch and pray so they would not fall into temptation (Matthew 26:41). When you pray with a focus on exposing and defeating deception, you partner with God's divine justice. Prayer becomes a tool to confront lies, whether they come as confusion, fear, or false identities that try to bind you or others. Declaring God's truth against the lie is critical, and aligning your prayers with scripture amplifies their power. For example, praying verses like John 8:32—You will know the truth, and the truth will set you free—can break the chains of deception. Engaging in such targeted, passionate prayer positions you at the forefront of spiritual warfare, where victory is claimed through divine intervention and divine justice is established firmly in your life and community.

Keep in mind that this kind of prayer isn't passive; it requires persistence and a warrior's attitude. Consistently placing yourself before the throne, asking the Holy Spirit for revelation about areas of deception, and decreeing divine justice creates a spiritual momentum. It's also helpful to pray with others who share your faith, forming a collective force fighting on the same front. When combined with a declaration of God's authority, these prayers become a formidable barrier against spiritual attacks meant to distort and deceive. Remember, the enemy's greatest desire is to keep people deceived and damaged, but your targeted prayer acts as a divine scalpel—cutting through lies and exposing truth, restoring what deception has stolen and establishing justice in every area of your life.

Creating a prayer routine that becomes part of your daily life is essential for maintaining victory over setbacks, deception, and spiritual fatigue. When you develop a consistent prayer lifestyle, it becomes a source of ongoing strength, equipping you to face new battles with confidence. Start by setting aside specific times each day dedicated solely to prayer, whether early morning, midday, or evening. Consistency turns prayer from a last resort into a first response—it becomes your spiritual armor that girds you up when challenges arise. Over time, this habit builds resilience, making you less susceptible to discouragement or despair, especially when life feels overwhelming. A sustained prayer life anchors your heart in God's presence, reinforcing faith and clarity amidst chaos.

Another vital aspect is cultivating a posture of openness and honesty before God. When you approach prayer not as a formal ritual but as an intimate conversation, it nurtures authentic connection. Share your struggles, express your fears, and ask for divine insight and strength. Incorporate praises and thanksgiving as well, which shifts your focus from problems to God's goodness. Writing down prayer requests and testimonies can help track your spiritual journey, reminding you of answered prayers and victories along the way. This practice of journaling deepens your understanding of God's faithfulness, empowering you to persevere during dry seasons or prolonged battles. It also encourages a mindset of constant dependence on God's grace, fostering a resilient prayer lifestyle that sustains your victory in Christ.

Implementing strategic prayer methods such as praying in the Spirit, using spiritual warfare declarations, or engaging in prayer walks can further strengthen your spiritual muscles. Prayer becomes not just a devotional act but a lifestyle of authority and trust. Building community through prayer groups or accountability partners provides mutual encouragement, especially crucial for those recovering from loss or setbacks. As you pray regularly, you develop spiritual reflexes—an instinct to reach out for divine help whenever needed. This ongoing relationship with God keeps your faith vigorous, transforming your outlook from survival mode to a victory mindset. Remember, a prayer lifestyle is about consistency, relationship, and expectant faith—that the God who hears will also answer and sustain you through every challenge.

Finally, never underestimate the power of perseverance in prayer. When obstacles arise or answers seem delayed, hold onto the promise that prayer is cultivating divine timing and alignment. Persistent, faith-filled prayer is often the key that unlocks breakthroughs in moments of silence or seeming delay. By maintaining an active, intentional prayer life, you establish a rhythm of victory that becomes part of your identity. This continuous communion with God fortifies your spirit, empowers your walk, and keeps you rooted in divine truth, ensuring that your spiritual strength remains unshakable despite circumstances. Keep praying, keep trusting, and never forget that your consistent voice in prayer acts as a shield and sword in the battle for your destiny.

The Authority of the Believer

Understanding the authority given to believers by Christ is foundational to living a victorious life. When Jesus defeated death and rose again, He didn't do so for Himself alone but for all who believe in Him. This authority isn't just a spiritual concept; it's a divine right that believers are called to claim and walk in daily. Declaring this authority isn't merely a verbal act; it's a confident, unshakable stance rooted in faith and understanding of who you are in Christ. When you speak with authority, you recognize that you have been equipped by God's power to stand against darkness and claim your divine inheritance.

This authority allows you to speak to circumstances, to decree what shall be, and to stand firm in God's promises. It begins with a conscious acknowledgment of what Jesus has already done for you: defeated every power of darkness and established you as an heir of the kingdom. You have the legal right to speak boldly, knowing that your words carry divine power. Scriptures such as Matthew 28:18-20 remind us that Jesus was given all authority in heaven and earth, and in His name, believers are authorized to operate in that same power. Walking in this authority requires intentional declaration—speaking God's Word over your life and circumstances—and resisting doubt or fear that might try to diminish your faith.

To claim your inheritance, start each day by declaring who you are in Christ. For example, confess: "I am a child of God; I am seated with Christ in heavenly places; I have authority over every work of the enemy." This isn't about wishful thinking, but about aligning your words with God's truth. When you speak God's Word with authority, it becomes a weapon against doubt and oppression. As you do so consistently, you'll begin to see situations shift as heaven responds to your declarations. Walking in this authority also means taking active steps—standing firm in prayer, resisting fear, and refusing to accept defeat. Remember, your words are powerful, and your declaration releases divine authority into your circumstances.

Your identity as a child of God is the foundation for walking in authority. It's easy to forget who you are when life hits hard, but understanding and embracing your divine identity transforms how you respond to challenges. You are not a victim of circumstances; you are a victorious heir, chosen by God and equipped for victory. Confidence in this identity empowers you to stand firm despite setbacks or pain. When you know you are loved unconditionally and accepted completely, you no longer need external validation to affirm your worth. This inner assurance becomes your shield against the lies of the enemy that try to diminish your worth or make you doubt your inheritance.

Standing confidently means declaring your identity with conviction and refusing to accept anything less than God's best for your life. Scriptures like 1 John 4:4 remind us, "Greater is He that is in you than he that is in the world." This isn't just a comforting verse but a declaration of your inheritance—your divine right to overcome. When doubts or fears surface, remind yourself of who you are in Christ: a redeemed, loved, victorious daughter or son of the Most High God. Embrace your calling, wear your spiritual armor, and walk boldly knowing that your identity in Christ grants you authority over every spiritual and natural obstacle.

Building this confidence requires daily renewal of your mind through Scripture and prayer. Speak out loud who you are in Christ, declaring victory and reminding yourself of God's promises. Over time, this affirmation deepens your sense of spiritual authority and shifts your perspective from defeat to victory. Remember that being confident doesn't mean arrogance but a humble understanding rooted in God's Word. As you walk in your identity, you will naturally begin to see divine opportunities open up and doors of breakthrough swing wide. Your confidence in Christ transforms your mindset from one of weakness to one of power, love, and a sound mind, making it easier to stand firm against any attack or setback.

6// BREAKING GENERATIONAL AND SOUL TIES

Identifying Unhealthy Spiritual Bonds

Unhealthy spiritual bonds, often called soul ties, are connections that create spiritual, emotional, and even physical bondage, preventing believers from fully walking in the purpose God has for them. These ties are more than just human relationships; they are spiritual links that can be formed through shared trauma, manipulation, broken vows, or toxic attachments. Many women in faith communities who have endured loss, disappointment, or deception unknowingly carry these burdens, which can distort their view of themselves, their worth, and their divine destiny.

These bonds can look like lingering emotional dependencies on former partners, manipulative friendships that drain spiritual strength, or even lingering resentments rooted in past heartbreak. Over time, such ties entangle and entrap the believer, making it difficult to hear God's voice clearly or pursue the set path He has prepared. The effects are often subtle at first—feeling tired, spiritually numb, or disconnected from God's presence—and gradually, these feelings can deepen into spiritual stagnation or recurring cycles of hurt and disappointment.

Scripture clearly warns against such attachments, emphasizing the importance of discernment. For example, in 2 Corinthians 6:14, Paul encourages believers not to be unequally yoked with unbelievers, which underscores the importance of guarding the spiritual relationships we allow into our lives. Recognizing these unhealthy bonds requires spiritual sensitivity and honest reflection because our natural eyes may overlook the depths of manipulation and control lurking beneath surface appearances. To truly move forward into God's plan, believers must learn to identify and break free from these destructive ties, realigning themselves with God's truth and purposes.

They often manifest through recurring patterns of codependency, feelings of obligation toward toxic individuals, or signs of spiritual oppression, such as persistent fear, shame, or confusion. Identifying these ties isn't about judgment but about spiritual clarity—recognizing what hinders your walk and disrupts your peace. This process involves prayer, examining your relationships through biblical truth, and seeking the Holy Spirit's guidance to reveal the cords that bind you unfairly.

Identifying these bonds also means understanding that some connections may have been formed during vulnerable moments or under deceptive circumstances, making it crucial to approach the process with humility and grace. It's not about blame but about acknowledging where the enemy has impeded your divine path. Once recognized, the next step is to confront these ties with faith, knowing that God's Word offers freedom and victory over every form of bondage that seeks to hinder your divine purpose.

Spiritual discernment is a gift from God that allows believers to see beyond superficial appearances into the spiritual realities operating around and within them. Asking God for clarity to identify which relationships, thoughts, or attachments are unhealthy is vital in breaking free from soul ties. Prayer becomes the spiritual antenna through which God reveals hidden influences or spiritual strongholds that might otherwise go unnoticed. When praying for discernment, it's essential to approach God with humility, faith, and a desire for truth, trusting that the Holy Spirit will illuminate the areas that need attention.

Effective discernment starts with sincere prayer, asking God to reveal any unholy or hindering attachments. Philippians 1:9-10 emphasizes the need for love mixed with knowledge and discernment, so believers can approve what is excellent and be pure and blameless. As they pray, they should also listen quietly, waiting on God's Spirit to confirm truths or reveal areas of spiritual compromise. The Holy Spirit can often point out subtle influences, like persistent negative feelings, recurring patterns of destruction, or attachment to people who distort your spiritual growth.

In practical terms, praying for discernment involves specific steps. First, confess and repent of any known sins or areas of vulnerability. Second, ask God to bring to light any unholy relationships or bonds that are preventing His full plan from manifesting. Third, seek wisdom and insight through Scripture, comparing your relationships and feelings to biblical principles. Sometimes, God will give you a specific scripture, a phrase, or an impression that acts as a spiritual warning. Journaling your prayers and God's revelations helps solidify what He's showing you and prepares you to take the necessary steps for spiritual freedom.

Remember, spiritual discernment isn't a one-time event but a continual process. Habits of prayer, meditation on God's Word, and submission to the Holy Spirit's leading keep your spiritual eyes open. This ongoing discernment process empowers you to recognize bonds as they form and gives you the spiritual authority to break ties that impede your progress. As you trust God's guidance, you gain not only clarity but also confidence that He is actively restoring and healing every area of your life that has been affected by unhealthy connections.

Part of walking in discernment is trusting that God's timing is perfect. He may reveal certain ties only after you've begun the process of prayer and confession. Be patient and persistent, knowing that spiritual freedom is a journey. Sometimes, breaking free involves practical steps like setting boundaries, cutting off toxic relationships, or seeking counsel from a trusted spiritual father or mother. Always remember that God's power is greater than any bondage, and through prayer, obedience, and faith, you can experience true liberation and step fully into the destiny He has planned for you. One practical tip is to keep a prayer journal of your spiritual discernment journey, documenting what God reveals and your responses, so you can track your progress and stay encouraged along the way.

Renouncing and Releasing with Authority

Many believers carry unseen burdens rooted in family lineages—patterns of dysfunction, addiction, fear, or destructive habits that seem inherited without explanation. These are often referred to as generational curses, which are spiritual chains passed down from previous generations. Recognizing that these curses are real and powerful is the first step toward breaking free. When you stand in the authority of Jesus Christ, you can declare decisively that those curses no longer have authority over your life. Using His mighty name, you can renounce these familiar spirits, patterns, and holdovers from your ancestors, understanding that Jesus defeated every work of darkness at the Cross. This act of renunciation is not just symbolic—it's a declaration of spiritual sovereignty, rooted in scripture like Galatians 3:13, which reminds us that Christ redeemed us from the curse of the law. Making this declaration out loud, with faith and conviction, invites God's power into your situation and begins to dismantle the invisible grips that try to hold your family line hostage.

Renouncing generational curses involves a deliberate, faith-filled prayer that specifically names the curses or issues you believe are afflicting your family or your own life. For example, you might declare, In the name of Jesus Christ, I break every curse of poverty, sickness, addiction, or fear passed through my bloodline. I declare that this curse has no authority over me or my descendants. It is vital to approach this with faith, knowing that Jesus' finished work on the Cross is sufficient to set you free from all bondage. Confirm your authority as a believer, understanding that because you are in Christ, you have the power to command curses to break and be dissolved. It is also helpful to ask the Holy Spirit to reveal any hidden areas where curses may be lurking so you can address them specifically. Remember, spiritual authority is exercised through spoken words paired with unwavering belief that Jesus has already won the victory over darkness.

Once curses are renounced, the next crucial step is to declare liberty and freedom over your life. Speaking these words aloud is an act of ownership, claiming the fullness of what Jesus paid for—freedom, peace, and restoration. You are not just asking for release; you are commanding it to manifest in your experience, aligning your words with God's promises. Declare freedom from any invisible chains, soul ties, or spiritual entrapments that attempt to cling to your identity or affect your destiny. By boldly speaking liberty over your life, you are breaking the power of any negative influence, addiction, or bondages that try to hold you captive. The words you speak are vehicles of spiritual authority; when rooted in faith, they become divine decrees that set the spiritual atmosphere for breakthrough. This is not merely speaking wishful words but declaring prophetic truths based on God's Word, such as Galatians 5:1, which states that Christ has set us free—so stand firm and do not let yourself be burdened again by a yoke of slavery.

Practical steps in declaring liberty include choosing precise, positive affirmations that reflect your desired outcome. For example, "I declare that I am free from every spirit of fear, depression, and rejection. I speak liberty over my mind, my heart, and my body. I am no longer bound by the chains of my past; I am a new creation in Christ Jesus." As you speak such declarations, combine them with faith and thankfulness, recognizing that your words carry authority in the spiritual realm. It's also helpful to visualize oneself stepping into freedom, imagining the chains breaking apart and seeing oneself walking in peace and wholeness. Making a habit of this declaration each day keeps your heart focused on God's promises, reinforcing your identity in Christ and strengthening your spiritual stance against any lingering influences. Remember, declaring liberty is not only about breaking chains but also about claiming God's truth and walking confidently in your redeemed identity.

How to Enforce God's Promises Like a Legal Right

The Courtroom of Heaven Is Not Moved by Tears — It's Moved by Truth

It was a painful season. Betrayal had come not from a stranger, but from a trusted partner. Kell's name was on contracts, but the money never came. Meetings were held, but she was excluded. Her voice was silenced. Her dignity was bruised. By the time the truth emerged, the damage was deep—financially, emotionally, spiritually.

She prayed. She cried. She begged. But it felt like God was silent. Until one day, kneeling at 3:12 a.m., she heard deep in her spirit:

"You're not waiting on me. I'm waiting on you to bring your case to the court of Heaven."

She rose from that place, dried her tears, and pulled out her journal. Instead of rehearsing the pain, she began **documenting the promises**.

Spiritual Law vs. Emotional Release

God is compassionate. He sees our tears. But in spiritual warfare, tears aren't enough.

The enemy is a *legalist*—he will exploit ignorance. But he cannot ignore *written law*.

"Put Me in remembrance; let us argue our case together; state your cause, that you may be proved right." – Isaiah 43:26 (NASB)

This is not emotionalism. This is **spiritual litigation**.

The Real-Life Turnaround

Kell didn't just cry. She documented:

- The money lost
- The promises broken
- The relationships that imploded
- The emotional and spiritual labor invested

But on the other side of the page, she began writing **God's Word**:

"The wealth of the wicked is laid up for the just." (Proverbs 13:22)

"I will restore to you the years the locusts have eaten." (Joel 2:25)

"If the thief be found, he must repay sevenfold." (Proverbs 6:31)

That journal became her *petition* in Heaven's court.

She sowed a seed in faith, not to manipulate God, but to **sign her case with action**. Within months, deals were reversed. Unexpected restitution came. A new stream of clients opened. But the real reward wasn't the money—it was the **authority she gained** from understanding that God's promises are not just poetic—they are **legal rights**.

ACT OF ACTIVATION

You don't get back what you lost by being emotional.

You get it back by being *legal* in the Spirit.

Declare this:

"I am not begging—I am legislating.

I am not weeping—I am winning.

God's promises are mine by covenant.

I will not back down. I am taking it back!"

KEYS TO ENFORCING SPIRITUAL LAW

Gather the Evidence

List your losses, but then *match them with Scripture*. Find the legal basis in the Word for your restoration.

File Your Case in Prayer

This isn't a casual "Lord, help me." This is intentional, scripture-backed prayer. Present your case like a legal petition.

Seal It with a Seed

A seed is not payment—it's prophetic alignment. It says, "God, I believe You so much, I'm willing to put action behind my faith."

Speak Your Verdict

Heaven waits for your decree. The enemy cannot hold what Heaven has released. Declare your "Get Back" daily.

"You will also decree a thing, and it will be established for you; and light will shine on your ways." – Job 22:28

ENCOURAGEMENT

Beloved, don't let your feelings override your faith. God isn't asking for emotion—He's asking for boldness.

"Let us therefore come boldly unto the throne of grace…"
– Hebrews 4:16

Step into the court.

State your case.

Declare your right.

Take it back.

"The seed you plant now represents not just faith, but expectation."

In the natural world, you don't sow a seed and forget about it — you **expect a harvest**. You water it. You watch for it. You *prepare* for it. So why would we sow spiritual seeds without that same expectation?

FAITH IS WHAT PLANTS IT — EXPECTATION IS WHAT GROWS IT

Let's go deeper:

- **Faith says,** *"God is able."*
- **Expectation says,** *"God is already moving."*
- **Obedience says:** *"I'm activating it NOW."*

That seed—whether it's time, prayer, finances, obedience, or worship—is more than an offering. It's a **spiritual transaction**. When you release it in faith, you're saying to Heaven:

"I'm not just hoping. I'm expecting Heaven to respond. I have the legal right to the harvest."

BIBLICAL PRINCIPLE

"While the earth remains, seedtime and harvest, cold and heat, summer and winter, day and night, shall not cease."

– Genesis 8:22

This verse isn't just about farming—it's about *spiritual law*. Seed always brings harvest — if it's planted in **faith and expectation**.

REAL-LIFE CONNECTION

A single mother sowed a small seed during a church fast, not because she had extra, but because she had a prophetic word hanging over her life. She wrote *"debt cancellation"* on that envelope. Within 30 days, a debt she thought would take years to pay was **wiped out** through an unexpected financial award.

It wasn't about the amount.

It was about the **expectation** she wrapped around that seed.

DECLARATION TIME

"My seed is not silent. It's speaking in Heaven.

I'm not just believing — I'm expecting.

I'm not sowing in fear — I'm sowing for favor.

And I will see my GET BACK in full."

"I'm getting my POWER back.

I'm getting my JOY back.

I'm getting my MONEY back.

I'm getting my LIFE back.

Enemy—you're gonna have to STEP BACK because I'm stepping INTO my divine season!"

Embracing Holiness and Identity in Christ

Understanding who you are in Christ begins with recognizing your divine status as a vessel set apart for God's purposes. Many women in faith communities carry wounds from past hurts, setbacks, or even deception that have dulled the clarity of their true identity. Yet, Scripture declares in 2 Corinthians 5:17 that anyone in Christ is a new creation; the old has passed away, and all things have become new. This means that no matter how broken or lost you may feel, your identity is rooted in the righteousness of Jesus, which makes you holy and pure before God. Walking in this truth requires intentional renewal of your mind, replacing every lie of the enemy with God's word that affirms your holiness. Every time you face doubts or accusations, remind yourself that Christ's blood has made you acceptable in God's sight, a vessel worthy to carry His presence. Embracing this identity isn't about perfection but about acknowledging who you are in the spiritual realm—chosen, loved, and called to live in righteousness. When you see yourself through God's eyes—clean, redeemed, and empowered—you step into a new level of authority to resist temptation and walk confidently in the righteousness that Christ has provided. Remember, your holiness isn't based on your feelings or circumstances but on the unwavering truth of Scripture that you are set apart for divine purpose.

Reclaiming this divine identity involves actively choosing to believe what God says about you and rejecting the lies that the enemy plants concerning your worth or past. It's a declaration of faith that transforms how you carry yourself daily. This process entails meditation on God's Word, prayer for clarity and strength, and fellowship with others who affirm your identity in Christ. As you do this, ask the Holy Spirit to help you see yourself with spiritual eyes and to heal the wounds that threaten to distort your view of yourself as a holy vessel. The more you remind yourself of God's promises, the more you will walk in righteousness and purpose. Remember, living as a vessel of holiness impacts not only your life but also positions you as a leader and example in your community. Your life becomes a testimony of God's transforming power, shining His light into dark places, and inspiring others to step into their true identity with confidence and grace.

Understanding your divine purpose begins with fully embracing your identity in Christ, knowing that He created you with specific plans and divine assignments. Many women have faced setbacks or broken periods in life that have caused them to forget or doubt their purpose. The enemy works tirelessly to whisper lies that your past disqualifies you or that you're insignificant. However, Scripture affirms in Ephesians 2:10 that we are God's handiwork, created in Christ Jesus for good works that He prepared beforehand. When you accept this truth, you recognize that your life has a divine design that goes beyond your circumstances or failures. Embracing your identity in Christ means aligning your heart with His purpose, seeking His direction through prayer, and listening to the Holy Spirit's promptings. It involves removing the labels of shame or despair and replacing them with declarations of God's plans for abundance, enablement, and impact. Your true purpose is not merely about what you do but about who you are in Christ—a reflection of His love, grace, and righteousness that was destined before the foundation of the world.

Walking boldly in your divine purpose requires intentional steps to identify the unique calling God has placed on your life. Start by asking God to reveal His specific plan for you, and then be attentive to the signs and opportunities He provides. Sometimes, this means stepping out of your comfort zone, forgiving those who have wronged you, and releasing past disappointments that blind you from seeing your divine potential. Don't rush the process; patience in waiting on God deepens your understanding and prepares you for the next season. Partner with mature believers or mentors who can encourage you and confirm your divine assignments, helping you recognize opportunities for service and influence. Living in this joyful awareness shifts your perspective from survival to purpose-driven living, allowing you to walk confidently, knowing that your life is set apart for God's glory. As you embrace your identity in Christ, you'll find that purpose becomes clearer, more focused, and filled with the power to transform not only your life but also those around you. Remember, your purpose is a reflection of God's love through you, revealed when you live authentically as His beloved child."

7. FAITH-BASED RESTORATION PROCESSES

Aligning Your Faith with God's Word

Aligning your mindset and daily actions with God's Word is the foundation for experiencing true restoration. When life has hurt you deeply, it's common to feel defeated or lost, but God's promises remain available to those who choose to walk in faith and obedience. The process begins by renewing your mind, replacing negative thoughts with God's truths—reminding yourself that His plans for you are good, and His mercy endures forever. As you meditate on scriptures like Isaiah 61:7, which speaks of your double portion, you start to shift your perspective from sorrow to hope. This mental alignment fosters a spiritual environment where divine restoration can be activated, breaking the chains of despair that pain often imposes.

Yet, aligning your thoughts isn't enough if your actions contradict God's principles. Walking out your faith involves taking steps that reflect your trust in God's promises. This could mean forgiving those who have hurt you, releasing resentment, and choosing love over bitterness. In practical terms, it may involve breaking free from unproductive habits, confessing your struggles to trusted believers, and actively pursuing righteousness. When your actions demonstrate obedience and surrender, you set a pathway for God's power to move in your circumstances. Remember that consistent obedience invites divine intervention—it's the bridge that connects your faith to tangible breakthroughs, resetting your life back on God's divine timetable for restoration.

In this process, don't overlook the importance of community and accountability. Surround yourself with spiritual mentors and brothers and sisters in faith who can encourage you, pray with you, and help keep your focus aligned with God's Word. Prayer becomes a crucial tool, allowing you to reaffirm your commitment and invite divine guidance. Declare God's promises aloud; speak His Word over your situation because words carry divine authority. As you declare His truth, you activate spiritual forces that restore not just your circumstances but also your inner being. Remember, the act of aligning your thoughts and actions is ongoing—a daily choice to stand firm in faith, even when doubts creep in. Stay committed to this alignment, and watch how God begins to orchestrate your restoration with purposeful precision.

Speaking God's Word over your life is a powerful weapon that releases divine energy into every area of your existence. Confession is not just about saying words; it is about believing in your heart that what you declare matches God's truth and that He will bring it to pass. Consistent confession helps reprogram your mind, replacing doubts and fears with faith-based declarations rooted in scripture. When you proclaim passages like Psalm 103:2-4 or Jeremiah 29:11, you're aligning your voice with heaven's voice, creating an open channel for God's power to move on your behalf. This habitual declaration becomes a pattern of faith that builds expectancy, fortifies your spirit, and keeps you focused on God's promises instead of your setbacks.

Breakthrough often begins with your words. Faith is activated when you confidently declare God's Word over your circumstances. It's helpful to pick specific scriptures that relate to your situation—whether you're believing for healing, provision, or emotional restoration—and repeat them regularly. For example, declaring, "I am more than a conqueror through Christ," reminds your soul of your divine identity and reminds Heaven that you are in agreement with God's victory. This spiritual discipline creates an atmosphere where doubt begins to fade, and hope rises. Writing these declarations down and speaking them aloud every day can reinforce your faith and serve as a constant reminder that God's power is alive and active in your life.

Consistency is key. The enemy will often try to dilute your declarations with discouragement or doubts, but persistence in confessing God's Word will strengthen your faith muscles. It helps to establish specific times during the day for focused declarations, such as morning and evening. Use declarations not only for your personal healing but also for your family, community, and future. By keeping your mouth busy with God's promises, you create a spiritual environment where breakthroughs become inevitable. Remember that your words carry authority—so speak boldly and confidently. Over time, this consistent confession aligns your heart and mind with God's truth, dissolving strongholds and opening the way for divine restoration to manifest fully in your life.

Practicing Patience and Expectancy

Patience is more than just waiting; it's actively trusting that God's timing is perfect, even when circumstances seem delayed or confusing. When we face setbacks or feel abandoned by promises we believed were from God, it's easy to become restless or doubt His promises. Yet, scripture invites us to hold onto confidence while staying calm in the wait. Developing patience in this way requires a shift from focusing solely on the outcome to trusting in God's process. It's a conscious choice to believe that God's delay is not denial but preparation. As you meditate on scriptures like Habakkuk 2:3, which reminds us that the vision is for an appointed time, you can learn to align your expectations with divine timing. This means declaring over your life that God's word will come to pass, even if it takes longer than expected. Practicing patience becomes an act of faith, trusting that God's word will unfold at the right moment. It's also about remaining peaceful in your heart, resisting the urge to rush ahead or manipulate circumstances, knowing that God's response will be perfect and timely. Confidence in God's faithfulness grows stronger when you intentionally speak His promises over your life and refuse to settle in doubt or discouragement. Remember, patience rooted in faith forms a solid foundation that sustains you during times of waiting, transforming your perspective from frustration to hopeful anticipation.

Standing firm in this posture of patience requires actively expecting God's response without giving up. It's vital to prevent feelings of disappointment from overtaking your faith. Expectancy must be rooted in confident belief that God hears and answers prayer. As Hebrews 11:1 states, faith is the substance of things hoped for, the evidence of things not seen. With this mindset, you learn to keep your hope alive, even when the evidence appears obscure or delayed. Maintaining a watchful, prayerful attitude creates a spiritual atmosphere where God's promises can manifest. It's like planting seeds; you water them with faith and keep tending to them with expectation, knowing that at the appointed time, they will bloom. You can also adopt practical habits such as journaling your prayers and God's promises, reminding yourself of His faithfulness in past situations. Over time, these practices deepen your trust, making patience a natural expression of your faith rather than a burdensome obligation. Remember, God is never late—His timing is always perfect, and His responses are calibrated in love and wisdom. Confident expectation combines prayer, scripture, and unwavering trust, guiding you through the seasons of waiting with strength and peace.

Remaining steadfast in faith even when the evidence seems to contradict promises is one of the most challenging yet rewarding acts of spiritual warfare. Trusting God's process means believing that His ways are higher than ours (Isaiah 55:8-9) and that every delay has a divine purpose. It's about refusing to allow doubt or discouragement to shake your confidence in God's goodness. Instead, you stand firm in the truth that what God has spoken over you will come to pass in His perfect timing. Persisting in faith often requires continuous prayer, repeated declarations of God's promises, and deliberate holding onto hope despite external circumstances. This persistence is not stubbornness but an active stance rooted in trust. Consider how Abraham, against all odds, kept believing God's promise of a son despite waiting many years (Romans 4:20-21). His perseverance was fueled by unwavering trust in God's promise rather than by sight or feelings. Likewise, your faith walk involves pushing forward through setbacks, remembering that God's process is refining and shaping you for the blessings ahead. This process might involve lessons of humility, patience, or obedience—each a vital part of your spiritual growth. By standing firm and refusing to waver, you position yourself to receive what God has prepared, knowing that His process is perfect and purposeful.

Daily disciplines can help reinforce this persistence. For example, declare affirmations that align with God's promises, such as, I believe that God is working all things together for my good, or, God's timing will bring victory in my life. These declarations strengthen your faith and serve as spiritual anchors during challenging times. Cultivating a community of faith—whether through prayer groups, mentors, or church fellowship—can also support your perseverance. Sharing testimonies and encouragement reminds you that you are not alone in this journey. Remember, time reveals God's faithfulness, and persistence in faith accelerates your spiritual maturity. When doubts surface, counter them with scripture and testimonies of God's past faithfulness. In trusting God's process, you acknowledge that every setback is a setup for a greater comeback, and your unwavering trust will eventually give way to divine fulfillment."

Testimonies of Divine Repair

Witnessing how God intervenes in the lives of His children provides powerful proof that restoration is possible, even in the darkest moments. Many have faced profound loss—whether of relationships, health, dreams, or stability—and have been met with divine mercy that renews hope. These stories serve as living proof that God's power is not just theoretical but active and present, capable of turning shattered lives into testimonies of new beginnings. When we hear how others have navigated their pain and have come out shining, it stirs faith within us to believe that our own circumstances can also change. These testimonies often highlight the process: from despair to deliverance, from brokenness to wholeness, reminding us that God's restorative hands are at work in every season of life.

Hearing of God's miraculous acts can stir a sense of anticipation that what was once deemed impossible is entirely within His reach. Many testimonies include details of how prayer, faith, and persistence opened the door for God's intervention. One person might share how their financial ruin turned into a blessing after crying out to God, while another recounts how their marriage, nearly broken beyond repair, was restored through divine grace and commitment. These accounts challenge doubts and replace them with faith, showing us that God's repair is personalized and tailored to each situation. Sharing and meditating on these stories fuels hope, ignites courage, and encourages us to believe in the God of miracles for our own lives.

It is helpful to remember that these stories are not just for inspiration; they are confirmation that God's promises are real and that divine restoration is rooted in His unwavering love. Each testimony may differ in details, but consistently echoes the truth that God restores, rebuilds, and renews. Reflect on these stories often, especially when you face your own setbacks, and let them remind you that no brokenness is beyond the reach of God's healing hands. Sometimes, sharing these testimonies with others can also reinforce your own faith and foster a community rooted in hope and divine power.

Your story of God's intervention can unlock faith in someone else who is struggling with similar pain or doubts. When you choose to openly testify about how God has restored your life, you become a beacon of hope that encourages others to believe that their turn of divine revival is near. Sharing your testimony is not about showing off; it's about giving someone a glimpse of God's supernatural power working in tangible ways. It builds a bridge of trust, inspiring others to step out in faith, pray boldly, or wait patiently on God's timing. Every account of divine repair, no matter how small or large, serves as a message that God is capable of transforming even the most broken situations.

Being transparent and authentic when sharing your story enhances its impact. People can tell when you are genuine, and that authenticity breaks barriers of skepticism. Your testimony may involve moments of struggle, doubt, or pain, but highlighting God's faithfulness through it all will remind others that God's grace sustains us even in the hardest storms. You can share how prayer, community support, fasting, or simply trusting in God's timing played a role in your recovery. This can encourage someone who may feel overwhelmed or hopeless to take that first step towards faith, knowing they are not alone and that divine help is available.

Remember to frame your testimony with humility and gratitude. Acknowledge God's hand in your turnaround and give Him the glory. Your story can also include practical steps you took—such as seeking prayer, reading Scripture, or leaning on trusted friends—to inspire actionable faith. As you share, keep in mind that God's power is still active and His promises are still true. Your willingness to be transparent can spark a ripple effect, leading others to seek the Lord earnestly for their own restoration. By doing so, you participate in building a faith-filled community where hope is contagious and divine possibilities become real for everyone involved.

8. REBIRTHING CONFIDENCE AND SELF-WORTH

Replacing Lies with God's Truth

Many women carrying wounds from past pain or setbacks often carry hidden lies about who they are—lies that speak louder than God's truth. These false messages can seep into your mind gradually, convincing you that you are not enough, that your worth is tied to your circumstances, or that you've failed beyond hope. Recognizing these deceptive thoughts is the first step toward breaking free, but it requires honesty and bravery. Pay close attention to recurring messages that trigger feelings of shame, guilt, or despair—these are often rooted in lies. Write them down, because seeing them on paper makes it easier to confront what isn't true. Once you see these thoughts clearly, challenge them head-on by asking, 'Is this what God says about me?' and compare each lie with Scripture. For example, if the lie whispers that you are unworthy, remind yourself that God's Word declares you are fearfully and wonderfully made. Confronting these lies also means refusing to accept them as part of your identity and starting to speak God's truth over your life. It's essential to realize that these false beliefs didn't come from God but from the enemy's schemes to keep you defeated and disconnected from your true worth rooted in Christ. Replacing these lies with God's voice requires intentional action—renouncing doubt and replacing it with faith-based affirmations rooted in Scripture helps rewrite the story you've been telling yourself for too long. Take time daily to reflect on what the Word says about you—this process builds your spiritual armor and stabilizes your mind against the deception that tries to hold you captive.

Once you've identified the false narratives, it's time to turn up the volume on God's truth. Scripture is your most powerful weapon in this spiritual battle because it directly speaks against lies and affirms your identity in Christ. For instance, if feelings of worthlessness creep in, remember Ephesians 2:10—For we are God's handiwork, created in Christ Jesus for good works. This verse clearly states that you are intentionally crafted by God's own hands, not by accident or failure. If guilt or shame try to define your history, hold onto Romans 8:1—There is now no condemnation for those who are in Christ Jesus. Such promises serve as divine clarifications that your past mistakes do not determine your present worth. To set a sturdy foundation, commit to memorizing key Scriptures that address the lies you struggle with most. Write them on cards and meditate on them daily, especially when negative thoughts threaten to take root. Keep in mind that renewing your mind is a continual process; one that involves replacing lies with truth consistently. As you speak aloud God's promises, you begin to override every lie that seeks to diminish your identity, restoring your confidence to stand firm in who God says you are. Remember, spiritual warfare is won not only through prayer but also through the relentless declaration of God's truth over your life.

Fighting lies also involves understanding that feelings are not always facts. Many women find themselves feeling unworthy or broken because of setbacks or losses, but feelings can deceive and distort reality. Choosing to believe what God says about you instead of relying solely on how you feel is a vital part of spiritual resilience. When negative thoughts come, pause and ask the Holy Spirit for guidance in discerning whether the thoughts originated from God or from the enemy. Practice replacing negative self-talk by declaring Scripture-based affirmations aloud, turning your mind back to God's perspective. Over time, this habit rewires the way you process emotions and thoughts, making you less vulnerable to the enemy's lies. Remember that God's Word is living and active, sharper than any two-edged sword. It has the power to cut through deception and establish truth deep within your spirit. As you consistently confront lies with God's promises, you'll find your self-worth rooted more deeply in His love and power, rather than in circumstances or feelings that are fleeting and unreliable.

Building a Strong Inner Identity

Embracing your true identity starts with hearing the passionate declaration of God's love over your life. When you recognize yourself as God's beloved, you are anchoring your soul in a truth that can withstand any storm. This identity isn't something you have to earn; it's a gift bestowed by grace, purchased through Christ's sacrifice, and sealed by the Holy Spirit. Repeat to yourself daily, I am His beloved, because that declaration rewires your understanding of who you are. When doubts and accusations crash in, remind yourself of the cross — how Christ's love purifies and makes you new, turning wounds into stories of victory. Remember, this is not just a mental affirmation but a heartfelt declaration rooted in the scriptures that affirm your healed and victorious status. Walking in this truth transforms how you see yourself and how you face life's challenges, because a daughter who knows her worth in God's eyes refuses to be defined by setbacks or pain.

To fully accept and live out this divine identity, it's essential to confront any lies the enemy whispers—lies that say you are unworthy, broken, or defeated. Open your heart to God's Word, which speaks authority over your life. Scriptures like Romans 8:37 remind us that we are more than conquerors through Him who loved us. Personal testimonies serve as living proof of God's transformative power, confirming that healing and victory are possible for those who believe. As you begin to see yourself through God's eyes, your perspective shifts from self-pity and defeat to faith and declaration. This step is foundational in building a strong inner identity—knowing that you are loved unconditionally and that your story is already written in victory. Daily affirmations, prayer, and meditating on scripture will strengthen your inner voice, replacing the lies with God's truth, reinforcing who you truly are in Christ.

Confidence rooted in God's love also means trusting in His timing during seasons of difficulty. It's common to feel uncertain when life doesn't go as planned, especially after loss or setbacks, but these moments are opportunities to deepen your reliance on His promises. Remind yourself that God is not a man that He should lie; His word is sure. Celebrate small victories and breakthroughs as signs of His faithfulness, allowing them to build your trust step by step. Develop a habit of speaking confidently into your future, declaring the promises that align with God's word. As you do, affirmations like, God is working all things together for my good, become your declaration. Confidence isn't about pretending everything is perfect but about knowing that God's love and promises will carry you through, no matter how challenging the road looks. Begin to see yourself as confident and secure because you're held in the palm of your Father's hand, secure in His eternal word and unchanging love.

Walking in Discernment and Authority

Understanding and sharpening spiritual discernment is foundational for walking confidently in the authority God has given you. Discernment isn't just about recognizing right from wrong; it's about tuning into God's voice amid the noise of life, understanding His leadings, and differentiating His truth from deception. When you genuinely develop this spiritual sensitivity, you start to see yourself not as a victim of circumstances but as a vessel empowered by God's power and authority. This process begins with cultivating a close relationship with the Holy Spirit, who is the greatest guide in revealing divine truths. Prayer and meditation on God's Word become vital tools, helping to align your spirit with His voice and purposes. As you deepen your connection with Him, you begin to recognize His whispers amid the chaos, and your confidence in knowing your divine authority grows stronger.

Recognizing your divine authority requires you to understand what Christ's victory on the cross truly entails for your life. You are no longer powerless or defeated but positioned in Christ as a reigning queen, called to walk in power, love, and authority. Scripturally, Jesus declared, All authority in heaven and on earth has been given to me (Matthew 28:18). That same authority is accessible to you through faith and alignment with His will. When you discern God's voice and promises clearly, you agree with His Word over your circumstances, declaring His truth over your pain, loss, or setbacks. Discernment becomes a spiritual weapon that protects you from deception, helps you stand firm against fear or doubt, and ignites faith to act in alignment with God's promises. This practice transforms your understanding of your place in Christ, making you a confident bearer of His authority in every area of life.

Once you understand your divine authority, the next step is to walk in confidence, embracing the fullness of your identity rooted in Christ. Many women in faith communities struggle to fully believe who they are in Christ, sometimes overwhelmed by past hurts, setbacks, or feelings of inadequacy. Yet, your true identity is defined by what Jesus has accomplished, not by circumstances or mistaken labels placed on you. When you see yourself through God's eyes, you realize that you are chosen, loved, and called for specific purposes. Walking confidently means refusing to allow the enemy's lies to define you. Instead, you declare God's truth over your life daily, reinforcing your identity as a victorious, loved daughter of God. Developing this confidence involves intentionally renewing your mind with Scripture, remembering God's promises, and standing firm in your calling despite opposition.

Your calling is not limited to what you do but is deeply connected to who you are in Christ. It's about living out your purpose with clarity and boldness, knowing that you have been equipped for every good work. This might mean stepping out of comfort zones or confronting fears rooted in past failures, but your identity in

Christ gives you the strength to move forward. As you walk in this fullness, others are encouraged to see the grace and authority of God working through you. Your confidence attracts others who are hurting or lost, and your life becomes a testimony of God's power to transform. Remember, walking in your calling isn't about perfection but about faith and obedience. As you consistently align your heart to God's truth, your actions will reflect the authority and identity that are already yours through Christ.

To help maintain this confident walk, it can be empowering to establish daily declarations over your life. Speaking out God's promises anchors your heart in truth and reminds you of your divine calling and authority. Combining these declarations with intentional prayer and the commitment to live out your true identity creates a lifestyle where confidence becomes natural. Over time, this conviction will push back fear, dispel doubts, and replace them with a fearless declaration of who you are and what you are called to do. Taking practical steps—such as journaling your identity in Christ, memorizing scriptures that affirm your calling, or engaging in a community that uplifts your faith—can strengthen your confidence and help you walk boldly every day.

9. OVERCOMING FEAR, DOUBT, AND INSECURITY

Tearing Down Strongholds of Fear

Fear has a way of anchoring itself deep within our hearts, whispering doubts that hold us back from stepping into all God has planned. Often, these fears aren't obvious; they hide behind faces like shame, shame over past mistakes, the fear of failure, or the dread of being abandoned again after loss. Recognizing these fears requires honesty with ourselves. We must ask tough questions: What thoughts make my stomach tighten? When do I hesitate to move forward? Fear is not just an emotion; it's a spiritual force that clouds our vision and drains our hope. It whispers, You're not enough, or You'll never recover, becoming a barrier to trusting God's promises. Identifying the specific fears that grip us is the first step towards breaking free from them. It's about shining a light into the shadows of our hearts, exposing what we've kept hidden, and refusing to let these fears dictate our lives. Sometimes, it helps to write down what scares us, because seeing it clearly makes it less powerful. When we acknowledge the fears that paralyze us, we take back control and begin the process of dealing with them biblically and courageously.

Once we've identified the fears, it's essential to understand that they don't have the final say. Fear often takes root because of unresolved pain, deception, or a misunderstanding of God's character. For example, a woman who has suffered deep loss may fear trusting again, convinced that pain will never end. Another might fear that her past mistakes disqualify her from God's love, thinking she is beyond redemption. Recognizing these root causes helps us see that fears are not always about the present but often about distorted views of ourselves or God. We must remember that the enemy's strategy is to keep us bound by these false narratives, but Jesus came to set the oppressed free. We are called to stand firm in our identity as daughters of the King, and this begins by exposing every lie that fuels our fears. When the enemy whispers, "You will never recover," declare with boldness, "God is my healer, and His love never fails." Learning to face our fears openly allows God's truth to replace the lies, making way for faith to flourish once again.

The process of uncovering fears also involves understanding that they often stem from moments of hurt or betrayal. Healing begins when we confront these wounds rather than burying them deep inside. No matter how painful, bringing fears into the light allows us to surrender them at the cross. We must remember that fear's power diminishes when we choose to respond with Scripture and prayer. For example, reciting scriptures like 2 Timothy 1:7, "For God has not given us a spirit of fear, but of power, love, and a sound mind," reinforces our authority over fear. Building a habit of journaling our fears and then replacing them with God's promises can be a transformative step. It turns our focus from the amplified voice of fear to the clarion call of faith. Over time, recognizing and naming fears not only diminishes their grip but also unlocks the freedom to walk boldly in the plans God has for us, unhindered by doubts that once seemed insurmountable.

When fear attempts to take over, declaring God's love and His power becomes a spiritual weapon capable of dismantling every lie rooted in insecurity. The truth is, God's love is not just a gentle feeling but a powerful force that neutralizes fear. 1 John 4:18 reminds us, "There is no fear in love. But perfect love drives out fear, because fear has to do with punishment." Every time fear presents itself, we can respond by speaking aloud God's promises. Psalm 34:4 says, "I sought the Lord, and He answered me; He delivered me from all my fears." These declarations remind us that God's love is perfect and sufficient to handle our deepest worries. Declaring His power also involves reminding ourselves that nothing is impossible for Him. Luke 1:37 affirms, "For with God, nothing shall be impossible." When we declare these truths, we align ourselves with divine authority, giving space for fear to shrink and faith to grow. It's about choosing to believe more in the power of His love than in the strength of our fears. This act of declaration is not just words but a declaration of trust that shifts spiritual atmospheres and awakens hope in every broken piece of our hearts.

Standing firm in God's love means repeatedly confessing His promises until they become a natural part of our mindset. We can declare boldly that His love is enough to cover every wound and that His power is greater than any obstacle we face. Rehearsing scripture over and over helps embed our identity in His truth, casting out the lies that fear tries to embed within us. For example, declaring, "God's perfect love casts out all fear," transforms despair into hope. Creating a routine of declaring His Word out loud—especially in moments of anxiety—can shift a person's internal atmosphere from one of dread to peace. Remember, the battle against fear is fought in the spirit, and declaration is what sustains us. When you find yourself overwhelmed, declare His love and His power with conviction. It's through these verbal battles that faith is fortified, and fear gradually loses its grip. Trust that as you continue to speak His truths, you'll feel the heaviness of fear lift, replaced by a peace that surpasses understanding, rooted in confidence that nothing is stronger than your God's love and might.

Renewing the Mind with Scripture

Many believers find themselves caught in a cycle of doubt, especially when faced with setbacks, loss, or emotional pain. These negative thoughts can feel overwhelming, like a heavy fog that clouds your ability to see God's truth clearly. But the key to breaking free is to actively replace those doubts with Scripture that affirms God's promises. When doubts creep in, instead of dwelling on what seems impossible or uncertain, turn to the Word. For instance, if the enemy whispers that you're abandoned or forsaken, recall Psalm 27:10: Though my father and mother forsake me, the Lord will take me in. If doubts about your future surface, cling to Jeremiah 29:11: For I know the plans I have for you, declares the Lord, plans for welfare and not for evil, to give you a future and a hope. These promises are not mere words but anchors for your soul, grounding you in God's faithfulness and sovereignty.

Replacing doubt isn't about denying reality but about actively choosing God's perspective over fleeting feelings or false accusations. It requires mindfulness and intentionality, cultivating a habit of speaking Scripture aloud or meditating on it when negative thoughts arise. Keep Scripture cards close, memorize key promises, and declare them over your life during quiet moments and in the midst of chaos. Over time, these divine truths will become the lens through which you interpret every challenge, transforming despair into hope and fear into confidence. Remember, God's Word is sharper than any sword, capable of piercing through the fog and replacing it with truth. The more you feed your spirit with Scripture, the stronger your faith becomes in confronting doubts head-on, replacing every lie with God's unshakable truth.

Building a resilient and unwavering faith calls for consistent practice—the renewal of your mind each day. This isn't a one-time act but a lifestyle rooted in daily choices. Each morning, begin by intentionally submitting your thoughts to God's Word, making a conscious decision to focus on what is true, noble, and praiseworthy (Philippians 4:8). Take moments throughout your day to reaffirm God's promises, especially when doubts or fears surface. Repeating scriptures, journaling God's promises, or even singing worship songs that declare His faithfulness help ingrain these truths deep within. Just as physical muscles strengthen through regular exercise, spiritual muscles grow stronger through daily reinforcement of God's Word. Over time, this consistent renewal forms a new way of thinking—a mindset rooted in divine truths that withstands the storms of life.

Practicing daily renewal also involves eliminating negative influences that feed doubt, such as toxic relationships or draining media, and replacing them with faith-building resources. Develop a routine that includes reading Scripture, meditating on it, and speaking it aloud. For example, start each day by declaring, I am loved, protected, and provided for by my Heavenly Father, based on Romans 8:38-39 or Philippians 4:19. As you do this regularly, faith becomes less about effort and more about a natural response to God's word residing in your heart. It's through this habitual practice that your mind begins to shift, transforming your inner landscape from one of fear and insecurity to one anchored in confident trust. This unwavering faith isn't cultivated overnight but through persistent, intentional effort that aligns your thoughts with God's truth.

Make it a daily goal to read, meditate, and declare. Keep a journal of Scripture promises that speak directly into the areas where you struggle most. Review these promises often, especially during moments of temptation or discouragement. Over months and even years, this disciplined approach will reshape your mental landscape, helping you stand firm in the face of adversity and walk confidently in the fullness of God's promises. Faith is built brick by brick, and daily renewal acts as the mortar that binds each piece together into a resilient fortress, guarding your heart and mind against doubt and despair.

Stepping Out in Bold Faith

Living in bold faith requires choosing to step beyond our comfort zones, even when circumstances seem uncertain or intimidating. It's about leaning fully on God's promises, knowing that He is our provider and protector in every season of life. When we face financial difficulties, broken relationships, or personal setbacks, trusting in Him means releasing our grip on anxiety and clinging to His word that He will supply all our needs according to His riches in glory. This kind of trust isn't blind; it's rooted in the deep conviction that God's love and sovereignty surpass any challenge we encounter. Every time we take a step forward in faith, we affirm that our confidence isn't in our strength but in His power working through us.

One of the most powerful acts of faith is obeying God's call despite fear or past failures. For example, Abraham left everything familiar without knowing exactly where God was leading him. His journey teaches us that boldness begins with surrendering our plans and trusting that God's direction is perfect. When you face moments of doubt or temptation to hold back, remind yourself of God's character: He is faithful to protect and provide when we dare to trust Him fully. Setting aside fear means choosing to believe that God's protection covers you—even when you're walking through shadows—because His presence is your safeguard. Small acts of trusting God in daily life—whether forgiving someone, speaking truth, or stepping out in obedience—build spiritual muscles that grow stronger over time.

Living rowdily in the face of uncertainty is about actively demonstrating that your faith is alive. It involves taking risks—like reaching out to someone hurting, sowing seeds of kindness even when rejection seems possible, or making decisions that reflect God's promises rather than worldly doubts. Every step of faith becomes a declaration that you serve a God who is bigger than any obstacle. When you affirm God's provision, you create space for miracles to manifest; His resources begin to flow where you once saw scarcity. Remember, trusting God isn't a passive act but a courageous stance that invites His supernatural involvement in your life. As you set your sights on His promises, you position yourself to receive divine breakthroughs that can transform your story from despair to victory.

To live boldly as a conqueror is to embrace the truth that Jesus Christ has already defeated every force that seeks to harm, deceive, or discourage us. The cross is the ultimate declaration that triumph over death, sin, and every enemy has been secured. When we accept this truth, we no longer need to live under the weight of fear, shame, or defeat. Instead, we rise up daily with confidence, knowing that our identity as children of God is rooted in the victorious Christ. Every challenge becomes an opportunity to demonstrate that we are more than conquerors through Him who loves us. Living from this victory means refusing to let setbacks define us because we understand they are temporary—just parts of the enemy's attempt to undermine God's plan for our lives.

Walking as conquerors involves renewing our minds with God's Word, which continually reminds us of who we are in Christ. Scriptures like Romans 8:37 declare, "In all these things, we are more than conquerors through Him who loved us," giving us authority to speak against adversities. When we face discouragement or pain, recalling Jesus' triumph over the grave fuels our faith and empowers us to stand firm. This outlook shifts our perspective from being victims to being warriors, fully aware that Christ has already secured our victory. As we live boldly in this truth, our actions, words, and attitudes reflect a faith that refuses to be shaken, inspiring others around us to also stand firm in God's promise of victory.

Understanding that Christ's finished work on the cross is the foundation of our victory allows us to confront every destructive thought or situation with confidence. We begin to see defeats as opportunities for God's power to be displayed in our weakness. Our confidence is rooted not in human effort but in the unshakeable victory of Jesus. This realization enables us to move forward with a sense of authority, unafraid of setbacks because we know they are only temporary. Living as conquerors should influence every aspect of life—from our relationships to our work—because we are not fighting for victory but fighting from a position of victory already won. With every step, we declare that Christ's victory is ours and that His triumph over death and evil is the assurance that we can face anything the enemy throws our way.

When adversity strikes, remind yourself that God's power is made perfect in weakness. Maintain your focus on the finished work of Christ, and refuse to accept defeat as final. Instead, declare aloud that you are more than a conqueror, and act in accordance with that truth. Celebrate small victories as signs of God's power working through you. Keep your eyes fixed on Jesus, the author and finisher of faith, knowing that as you do, you are aligned with the ultimate victory that was won at Calvary. Cultivating a mindset of victory transforms how you face challenges, making each obstacle an opportunity to witness God's power and love in action.

10. ALIGNING WITH KINGDOM PRINCIPLES FOR RECOVERY

Stewardship and Faithfulness

Stewardship is more than managing what you have; it is a divine act of honoring God with every resource entrusted to you. When believers see their resources—be it finances, talents, or time—as gifts from God, their approach shifts from obligation to worship. Every dollar spent wisely, every moment invested intentionally, and every skill used for God's purpose becomes a demonstration of faithfulness. This mindset transforms daily living into a continual act of honoring God, reaffirming that our lives are not our own but belong to Him. Faithful stewardship requires ongoing discipline; it calls for regular evaluation of how resources are allocated and used, always aligning with God's principles and His kingdom's expansion.

Living as a faithful steward also involves understanding the spiritual significance of stewardship. It is rooted in recognizing that resources are seeds that can produce spiritual and eternal harvests. For example, giving generously in times of need not only supplies for practical needs but also manifests trust in God's provision. Managing time wisely empowers believers to do God's work effectively, serving others and advancing His kingdom. When stewardship becomes a form of worship, even the act of budgeting and saving carries spiritual weight—each decision made is an act of obedience. It's about trusting God to multiply our efforts, never seeing resources as mere possessions but as divine trust given for kingdom purposes. In practice, faithful stewardship involves daily choices that honor God, communicate trust, and demonstrate faithfulness in all areas.

Another vital aspect is developing a lifestyle of gratitude and humility, acknowledging that nothing truly belongs to us. Recognizing God's sovereignty over our resources encourages us to relinquish ownership and control, placing our trust fully in Him. This attitude not only shifts perspective but also releases burdens of greed or hoarding, which can hinder divine flow. When believers view their resources as tools to bless others and further God's work, they tap into a divine economy—one where blessing flows in response to faithful giving and responsible management. Practicing faithful stewardship requires intentionality, whether through regular prayer over finances, honest assessment of spending habits, or seeking God's guidance in decision-making. These acts knit our resources into acts of worship that produce spiritual fruit and align our lives with God's higher purpose.

Operating in integrity is fundamental to walking in divine increase. It involves more than honesty; it is about aligning every area of life with God's standards and being fully transparent before Him and others. God's principles for increase—such as sowing and reaping, diligent work, generosity, and obedience—are rooted in scripture and require believers to act consistently according to His Word. When we operate with fidelity to these principles, we position ourselves under God's favor and divine provision. Deception, dishonesty, or shortcuts might provide temporary gains, but they rob us of God's best and hinder divine flow. Faithfulness in small things, like faithful tithing or honest dealings, sets the foundation for greater blessings. The key is living with integrity, not just in public but within our hearts, for God evaluates both outward actions and inner motives.

Fidelity to God's ways is also a matter of guarding our hearts against compromised values and letting His Word guide every decision. It means resisting the temptation to manipulate situations for personal gain and instead trusting God's timing and methods. Operating in integrity is an act of worship—it declares to the spiritual realm that our trust is in God's principles and His divine economy. When believers commit to remaining faithful, even when it's inconvenient or costly, they open the door for God to pour out increase according to His perfect will. This fidelity creates a fertile ground for divine multiplication, as blessing follows obedience. It's about making a conscious choice daily to walk upright before God, reflecting His truth in every transaction and interaction. Such consistency builds spiritual authority and attracts God's favor for the increase that comes from His hand alone.

Living with integrity also means being transparent about resources, sharing openly with others, and honoring commitments. It involves honoring God through timely giving, avoiding greed, and trusting Him to supply all needs. This faithful approach ensures that increase is not just about accumulation but about spiritual growth and legacy. As with any divine principle, perseverance and discipline are required; the more consistent we are in operating in integrity, the more we position ourselves for overflow. God's promises of divine increase are activated when we align our lives with His precepts, trusting that He rewards faithfulness and uprightness. Faithfulness in handling resources cultivates a reputation of integrity, which God will use to open doors and pour out His blessings beyond what we can imagine.

In practicing these principles daily, believers find that divine increase becomes a natural outflow of their faithful obedience. Whether through honest dealings, faithful tithe, or wise management, each act rooted in integrity unlocks divine favor. It's a lifestyle that requires intentionality and a deep desire to please God in all we do. As we hold fast to His standards, we cultivate an environment where His blessing can flood our lives, producing fruits that last. Remember, divine increase is not merely about financial blessing; it encompasses spiritual growth, health, relationships, and everything that adds to the fullness of life in Christ. When faithfulness and integrity become the foundation, God's capacity to increase and multiply is limitless, echoing His promise that those who are faithful with little will be entrusted with much."

CHAPTER FOUR: DOUBLE FOR YOUR TROUBLE

The Oil Costs More Because the Glory Will Be Greater

You Paid a Price No One Saw

They saw the praise, but not the pain.

They saw the smile, but not the sleepless nights.

They heard your hallelujah, but didn't hear the sound of your silent battles.

You walked through loss.

You endured seasons where it felt like everything and everyone left you.

Your tears watered the soil of destiny, but your heart questioned:

"God… will it ever be worth it?"

And here is Heaven's answer:

"Instead of your shame, you shall receive a double portion…" – Isaiah 61:7

THE COMPENSATION SEASON HAS ARRIVED

You've been sowing in tears,

But now you're about to **reap in double joy.**

This is not just recovery — this is **reward**.

This is not just restoration — this is **recompense**.

This is not just healing — this is **honor for your hurt**.

God says:

"For everything the enemy touched, I'm commanding a twofold return.

For every sleepless night, I'm releasing supernatural rest and radical favor.

For every 'no' you received, I'm releasing a 'yes' soaked in my glory."

BIBLICAL FOUNDATION: THE JOB STORY

Let's revisit Job.

- He lost his health, his wealth, his children, and the respect of those around him.
  - Even his wife said, *"Curse God and die."*
    - But Job didn't stop worshipping.
      - He kept his posture in pain.

And then this happened:

*"And the LORD gave Job **twice as much** as he had before." – Job 42:10*

REAL-LIFE STORY: VANESSA'S MINISTRY LOSS LED TO GLOBAL EXPANSION

Vanessa led a women's ministry that grew from 10 to over 500. She poured in her time, money, and heart. One day, she walked into a meeting to discover she'd been voted out, without notice, without explanation, by people she trained and loved.

She wept for weeks. But then, something shifted. God said:

"I didn't let them take it — I let them reveal it was too small."

That betrayal pushed her to launch a global online mentorship program. Within one year, her reach expanded to 37 countries. She gained more influence than she ever had in that local space.

She didn't just bounce back — she **bounced higher.**

That's **double for your trouble**.

WHY THE OIL IS EXPENSIVE

We love the anointing, but we forget:

Oil only comes from crushing.

"You anoint my head with oil; my cup overflows." – Psalm 23:5

That overflow isn't random — it's **payment for pressure**.

The Double Comes With a Purpose

You're not just being restored for personal comfort.

You're being **repositioned** for kingdom impact.

"God's double portion is not just for survival—it's for **assigning you to nations**."

SUPPORTING SCRIPTURES FOR YOUR SEASON OF DOUBLE

- **Isaiah 61:7** – *"Instead of shame… double portion."*
- **Zechariah 9:12** – *"Return to your stronghold, O prisoners of hope; today I declare that I will restore to you double."*
- **Exodus 22:7** – *"If a thief is found… he shall pay double."*
- **Job 42:10** – *"And the LORD gave Job twice as much."*

Declare This Over Yourself Now:

"I decree the season of lack is over.

I declare that for every tear, I shall reap joy.

For every betrayal, I shall receive elevation.

For every loss, I shall receive **double**.

This is my divine compensation season, and I will not miss my moment!"

ACTIVATION: PREPARE FOR THE OVERFLOW

Write down your top three losses—areas where you've been hurt, rejected, or robbed.

"This is for my **double**. I am not sowing into pain — I'm sowing into promise. What was taken will be returned, and my future will overflow."

CLOSING WORD

Beloved, they didn't see what it cost you.

But Heaven has tracked every tear.

Every hour you stayed when others walked out.

Every gift you gave when you had nothing left.

Every sacrifice. Every silent battle.

God is about to make a public announcement of private restoration.

You're not just getting up.

You're getting up with **double strength**, **double honor**, **double doors**, and **double grace**.

Get ready for the overflow. Your trouble is about to pay you back in full.

Generosity as a Recovery Tool

Generosity is more than just giving material possessions or resources; it's a reflection of understanding that everything we have ultimately comes from God. When we choose to give cheerfully and willingly, we align ourselves with God's divine nature, which is rooted in giving and loving unconditionally. This act of generosity is a spiritual principle that opens doors for His favor to flow freely into our lives. Often, people focus on their circumstances—feeling limited, hurt, or discouraged—yet true generosity reminds us that our divine connection surpasses temporary setbacks. When you give out of faith, not out of obligation or guilt, you activate a powerful supernatural law: that God is pleased when His children freely bless others. This principle promises that as we sow generously, we open the heavens for restoration, healing, and multiplication. Think of it as planting a seed into fertile ground—what you sow in faith, God will multiply in ways beyond your understanding, bringing about divine recovery where it seemed impossible.

By embracing generosity as a core divine principle, you're stepping into a spiritual act that has the potential to transform your circumstances. Such giving isn't merely about money, but encompasses time, kindness, forgiveness, and offering encouragement to others. Each act of giving aligns your heart with God's heart, positioning you for divine response. It is through this act that you demonstrate trust in God's ability to restore and compensate for what has been lost. The Bible repeatedly underscores this truth—God loves a cheerful giver and promises that those who sow sparingly will reap sparingly, but those who sow generously will reap generously (2 Corinthians 9:6). This is not just about giving for the sake of giving but doing so with a genuine, joyful heart, knowing that God's favor and power are activated through your faith-driven generosity. Rest assured, this divine principle is a pathway to recovery, a shortcut to breakthrough, and an anchor for enduring hope amid loss or disappointment.

Believing in divine multiplication is foundational when practicing generosity as a recovery tool. It's not enough to give out of obligation; instead, giving should flow from a place of faith and expectation. When your heart is aligned with God's promises, you understand that your seed—whether it's finances, time, or acts of kindness—does not perish but is destined to be multiplied. This belief transforms your perspective from seeing your limited resources as something to hold tight to into a channel through which God's power can work. As you release your seed with joy, you declare that you trust God's word that He will make it grow beyond your natural capacity. Numerous testimonies of believers affirm that when they gave cheerfully and in faith, they experienced unexpected recoveries, multiplications, and breakthroughs that relieved pain, restored hope, and reestablished their lives.

Practically, this means relinquishing doubts and embracing a confident declaration that God's word is true. For example, you might say, "Lord, I give this seed freely, trusting You to multiply it for my good and Your glory." As you do this, keep your focus on God's promises rather than the circumstances. It's helpful to develop a habit of thanking Him in advance for the multiplication, as thanksgiving is a powerful act that releases faith into the unseen realms. Remember, God is a God of abundance, and His multiplication capacity far exceeds what we can think or imagine. Giving cheerfully is a clear act of trust that God's law of sowing and reaping is working in your favor. The more you release your faith through giving, the more you position yourself for divine restoration. It's as if every act of cheerful giving plants a spiritual seed that will harvest a greater measure of recovery, implying that no act of generosity is ever wasted or overlooked by heaven.

To strengthen your faith in divine multiplication, consider regularly revisiting God's promises in Scripture. Meditate on verses such as Philippians 4:19, which assures us that God supplies all our needs according to His riches in glory. As you do this, you reinforce your faith that God is able and willing to restore what has been lost. Practice giving with expectation, celebrate every act of generosity as a seed being sown into your future, and remain steadfast in your belief that God is a multiplier, multiplying your seed for recovery, healing, and blessing. This mindset creates a spiritual environment where hope flourishes, and every act of giving becomes a declaration of faith that impossible situations are about to turn around. Remember, in the spiritual economy, sowing is always matched with reaping—trust God to multiply your seed for divine recovery and tangible breakthroughs in your life.

God Is Not Denying You — He's Aligning You

She Should've Been Married by Now.

Kell was the kind of woman who did everything "right."

She honored God in her youth.

Served at her church faithfully.

Worked long hours and sacrificed her dreams for her family.

Waited on the Lord for the "right one."

Even turned down men who didn't match her spiritual values.

But the years passed… and passed… and passed.

She was 39 now.

Still believing.

Still praying.

Still alone.

What broke her heart wasn't just being unmarried. It was as if **God seemed silent**. Her prayers echoed back empty. And when others around her got married, it felt like the delay was personal. Like God forgot her. Like life passed her by.

Delay Feels Like Rejection, But It's Often Protection.

Kell didn't realize it at first, but behind her delay was not just a circumstance — it was a **spirit**. A demonic force was strategically assigned to **frustrate**, **stall**, and **distract** her from destiny.

This wasn't God's will.

It wasn't just "waiting."

It was **warfare**.

"We wrestle not against flesh and blood, but against principalities… against spiritual wickedness in high places." – Ephesians 6:12

When Delay Is Spiritual, Only Spiritual Weapons Can Break It

She went on a three-day fast. On the third night, she had a dream. In it, she saw herself in a long line. Everyone ahead of her was receiving blessings, keys, and assignments. When it was finally her turn, the person handing out the blessings looked confused and said:

"Your name was moved to the back."

She woke up in tears.

That morning, while reading the Word, her eyes fell on **Daniel 10:12-13**:

"Do not fear, Daniel. From the first day that you set your heart to understand... your words were heard, and I have come because of your words. But the prince of the kingdom of Persia withstood me for 21 days..."

It hit her like thunder: **God answered on the first day**, but **warfare delayed the delivery.**

The Delay Wasn't Denial — It Was Interception

Tanya stood up from her couch and said out loud, "This delay is broken! I will not stay in line for something Heaven already released!"

Recognizing the Spirit of Delay

The enemy uses delay to:

- ❖ **Make you question your worth**
- ❖ **Wear you out spiritually and emotionally**
- ❖ **Causes you to miss divine timing**
- ❖ **Tempt you into settling for less**

"Hope deferred makes the heart sick…" – Proverbs 13:12

Delay isn't just inconvenient — it's **destructive**. It erodes confidence and makes you settle. But God is declaring:

"No more delay."

"…There will be no more delay!" – Revelation 10:6 (NIV)

God's Verdict Is: TIME'S UP

What Kell realized — and what *you* must know — is this:

Delay has an expiration date.

When you rise in **faith**, **fasting**, **declaration**, and **seed**, you **reset divine alignment**. You cancel the enemy's stall tactics and activate *accelerated grace*.

Scripture Breakthroughs

- **Habakkuk 2:3** – *"Though it tarries, wait for it; because it will surely come, it will not delay."*
  - ➤ *Prophetic delay is not permanent delay.*
- **Joel 2:25** – *"I will restore the years…"*
- ➤ *God doesn't just give back time — He makes the lost time profitable.*
- **Amos 9:13** – *"The days are coming when the reaper will overtake the plowman…"*
- ➤ *This is **divine acceleration**—when what used to take years happens in weeks.*

Prayer of Breakthrough

"Father, I repent for aligning with delay. I break the covenant with stagnation, sabotage, and spiritual cycles of delay. By the blood of Jesus, I revoke every demonic permission that has caused my destiny to be hindered. Let every Prince of Persia blocking my release be destroyed. Angels of breakthrough, be released now on assignment. I decree and declare: The Spirit of Delay is BROKEN — and I will walk in my divine timeline, in Jesus' name. Amen."

ACTIVATION TIME: WRITE THE DELAY DOWN — THEN BREAK IT

Get your journal.

Write every area where you've experienced a delay:

- Relationships
- Business
- Health
- Family
- Ministry
- Finances

"This delay is broken. I'm stepping into divine acceleration. My wait is over — the Spirit of Delay has lost its hold!"

Encouragement:

Beloved, you are not forgotten.

You are not forsaken.

You are not late — the enemy just *tried* to lock your release.

But today, the Spirit of Delay is broken.

This is your get-back season, and what was held up is being handed over.

Walking in Obedience and Discipline

Living in obedience to God's Word is the cornerstone of experiencing His blessings. When a believer intentionally aligns daily choices with biblical principles, they create an environment where God's favor can flow freely. This involves more than just occasional church attendance; it requires a conscious shift in attitude, habits, and priorities to reflect God's statutes. For example, maintaining honesty in dealings, showing compassion to others, and practicing integrity are visible signs that one is committed to His commandments. As you walk in obedience, you're not earning God's love—His love is unwavering—but you're positioning yourself to truly recognize and receive the blessings He desires to pour out. Disobedience, even in small areas, creates barriers that hinder divine flow, as sin and compromise have a way of obstructing the blessings meant for His children. Consistently checking your heart, repenting when necessary, and asking the Holy Spirit for guidance helps keep your lifestyle in line with God's will. By doing so, you establish a foundation that invites divine favor, prosperity, and protection into every aspect of your life, especially in times of hardship or setbacks.

Remaining disciplined in spiritual practices is essential for anchoring yourself in God's promises and sustaining breakthroughs. Prayer becomes your direct line to the Father, a time to commune with Him, seek His direction, and declare His Word over your circumstances. Fasting, on the other hand, is a powerful act of surrender, demonstrating your seriousness in seeking divine intervention and clarity. Consistent acts of faith—whether sharing your testimony, forgiving others, or trusting God's timing—act as spiritual anchors during trying times. These disciplines are not burdens but gateways that cultivate spiritual strength, resilience, and clarity. For a woman battling disappointment or feeling broken, maintaining a disciplined prayer life reminds her of God's sovereignty and love, rekindling hope where despair once dwelt. It's also during these times that faith acts—obedient steps taken in spite of feelings—become tangible expressions of trust in God's promises. Such acts keep your spirit attuned to His voice and open your heart to receive renewed strength, direction, and clarity for the next season of your life.

11. NAVIGATING EMOTIONAL AND SPIRITUAL BREAKTHROUGHS

Recognizing When Breakthrough Has Begun

When a breakthrough begins to unfold in your life, certain signals start to show up within your heart and mind. You might feel a new sense of hope growing inside, even amid lingering doubts. This isn't about optimism alone but a deep inner knowing that God is at work, shifting things unseen. You may notice your thoughts becoming clearer, divine inspiration stirring your spirit, or a fresh sense of peace settling over your worries. These signs often come gradually, but the consistency of feeling lighter or more hopeful is a strong indicator that a breakthrough is happening. Emotional shifts like a release from heaviness, a reduction in fear, or a newfound ability to forgive past hurts also point to divine progress. Spiritually, you might sense a stronger connection with God, feeling prompted or directed by His Spirit in ways that align with Scripture. This is God's way of confirming that His promises are starting to take shape in tangible ways, even if outside circumstances haven't caught up yet. Recognizing these signs requires attentiveness; they are often subtle but profound nudges from heaven, designed to encourage you to keep pressing forward.

Another powerful indicator is the ability to see your situation from God's perspective instead of through the lens of despair or discouragement. When your heart shifts from feeling trapped to trusting God's timing and plan, you are beginning to recognize a breakthrough. You might also notice a desire to pray more fervently, scriptures becoming more meaningful, or an irresistible draw to worship. These are signs that your spiritual senses are awakening, alerting you that God's hand is moving behind the scenes. Watch for divine encounters—unexpected conversations, prayers answered in small, meaningful ways, or divine coincidences that align favorably. Such moments often serve as reminders that God is working on your behalf, unlocking doors that once seemed firmly shut. Embrace these signs, knowing they are chapter markers in your journey of renewal and divine intervention, meant to bolster your faith and strengthen your hope.

Remaining aware of God's activity in your life is crucial during the time of breakthrough. It's easy to get caught up in the rush of change and overlook how God is orchestrating every detail to bring His promises to pass. Developing a habit of gratitude keeps your focus on His goodness rather than on lingering problems or unresolved issues. When you pause to thank Him—whether through prayer, praise, or quiet reflection—you acknowledge His sovereignty and His active role in your story. Gratitude shifts your perspective from "what's missing" to "what I see God doing." It opens the spiritual eyes to recognize blessings, big and small, that signal progress. Being alert also means paying attention to internal shifts—trust replacing doubt, joy emerging where there was sadness, or patience growing where frustration once reigned. These subtle changes reinforce that God's hand is at work, even when the external world remains unchanged. Celebrate these moments; they are proof that a divine breakthrough has begun, and your faith is being crowned with evidence of His power.

Practicing thankfulness becomes a powerful weapon against discouragement. It keeps your heart tender to God's voice and receptive to His guidance. For example, consider journaling daily about the small victories or answered prayers, no matter how insignificant they seem. This practice trains your mind to recognize ongoing divine activity, creating a spiritual record of progress. Additionally, sharing testimonies with trusted friends or your faith community renews your confidence, reminding you that others are also witnesses to God's work. As you cultivate a posture of gratitude and awareness, you become more tuned in to God's daily presence. This not only strengthens your faith but also encourages others around you, often sparking a ripple effect of hope and divine breakthroughs in the community. Trust that each sign, every moment of gratitude, and every recognition of God's hand is part of the larger story of your healing and victory in Christ.

Remember, breakthroughs are seldom one-time events but ongoing processes woven into your spiritual journey. By remaining alert to signs and grateful for every expression of God's activity, you position yourself to fully receive what He is doing. This mindset invites a continual flow of divine favor and increases your capacity to recognize His faithfulness in real time. Keep your eyes open and your heart thankful, because this attitude unlocks more revelation and accelerates the manifestation of God's promises in your life.

Maintaining the Breakthrough Momentum

Staying in a posture of persistent prayer is essential after experiencing a breakthrough. It's easy to breathe a sigh of relief and assume the battle has ended, but the enemy often strives to come back stronger once you relax. Continued prayer keeps you connected to God's presence, aligning your heart with His will and reminding you that your victory is rooted in His power, not your strength alone. Praise becomes a weapon—a declaration of God's goodness and faithfulness—shaping the atmosphere around you and reinforcing your faith. Thanksgiving is a daily act of recognizing God's hand in every small detail of your life, anchoring your heart in gratitude and trust. These spiritual disciplines act as barriers that keep discouragement and doubt at bay, helping you remain rooted in God's promises and His ongoing grace.

Engaging in continuous prayer and praise isn't just about asking for more blessings; it's about cultivating a lifestyle that honors God's sovereignty. When you lift your voice in thanksgiving, you reaffirm the truth that every victory belongs to Him. Remember, breakthroughs are often linked to moments of divine intervention, but they are sustained through ongoing communion with God. A practical way to maintain this momentum is to set aside specific times during your day for prayer and worship—morning, noon, and evening—making it a natural rhythm rather than a sporadic activity. Personal songs of praise, scriptures, and simple thankfulness can serve as anchors whenever you feel your strength waning. This ongoing dedication to worship keeps your faith renewed and your spiritual eyes focused on the future, trusting God to continue working behind the scenes even when you cannot see it clearly.

It's also helpful to keep a journal of answered prayers and breakthroughs, recalling how God has shown up in your life. This builds your faith and fuels gratitude, which in turn ignites more praise and prayer. Use scriptures as declarations, such as Psalm 103:1-5 or 2 Corinthians 1:20, affirming that God's promises are yes and amen. When you remain in this posture, you create a spiritual environment where breakthroughs become a lifestyle rather than a one-time event. Be intentional about celebrating victories, big and small, with praise, ensuring your heart remains thankful regardless of circumstances. This attitude of persistent prayer, praise, and thanksgiving becomes a spiritual armor that not only protects your breakthrough but positions you for even greater victories ahead.

Walking in the aftermath of a breakthrough requires vigilance over what enters your heart and mind. Victory in Christ is precious, but the enemy will often try to sow seeds of doubt, discouragement, or deception to shake your confidence and pull you away from the faith that brought you through. Guarding your heart means choosing to meditate on God's truth rather than negative reports, harmful conversations, or past pain. It involves setting boundaries—limiting exposure to negativity, unhelpful influences, and even certain social media content that diminishes your hope or sense of peace. Protecting your mind means renewing it daily with scripture and uplifting thoughts, refusing to dwell on what memories or views stir anxiety or defeat.

Understanding that your heart determines your actions is key—what you allow to flourish there influences every decision you make. Regularly examine your thoughts and motives; ask whether they align with God's promises or long for the old familiar fears. Scripture reminds us in Proverbs 4:23 to guard our hearts diligently because from it flow the issues of life. Filling your heart with God's

Word and His praise creates a stronghold against discouragement. When negative thoughts creep in, replace them with declarations rooted in scripture: I am more than a conqueror (Romans 8:37), or The Lord is my shield (Psalm 3:3). Such affirmations serve as mental armor, helping you stay focused on God's victory. Listening to uplifting worship music or Scriptures on repeat can also reinforce your faith and drown out any voice of defeat trying to surface.

Moreover, surround yourself with faith-filled people who encourage your walk and remind you of God's promises. Community is a powerful tool in maintaining victory because shared faith ignites hope and accountability. Remember, walking in ongoing victory isn't about never experiencing setbacks but about how you respond to them—keeping your heart and mind protected from despair and setting your sights on God's sustaining grace. It's a daily choice to remain anchored in His Word and His promises, knowing that your victory is secured by Him. Developing a habit of repentance and renewing your mindset helps you stay humble and dependent on God's strength, which is essential to preserving your breakthroughs. Protecting your heart and mind is an act of worship—an ongoing declaration that victory belongs to Jesus, and your victory is assured in Him.

Giving God All the Glory

Sharing testimonies of victory is a powerful act that visibly proclaims God's sovereignty and His ability to turn despair into triumph. When you lift up stories of how God has fought for you in times of struggle, it serves as a declaration that His power is unmatched and His ways are higher than ours. These testimonies do more than encourage—they shake the heavens and remind others that God's hand is not shortened, that His promises are true, and that His strength can be trusted in every season. By recounting specific instances of breakthrough, healing, provision, or restoration, you set in motion a spiritual atmosphere that attracts the mighty works of God into your life and community. Personal stories of victory are like arrows shot into the spiritual atmosphere, releasing faith and expectation among believers, even those who may feel overwhelmed or defeated.

When you openly declare these victories, consider framing them as acts of worship—testifying not just to inform but to honor and glorify God's power. Use scripture to validate your stories, grounding your testimonies in God's Word, such as Psalm 66:16, which calls believers to come and hear, all you who fear God; let me tell you what he has done for me. This not only affirms God's sovereignty but also shifts the focus from human effort to divine intervention. Remember, every victory is a signpost pointing back to God's glory, a living testimony of His ability to bring light into darkness. Sharing these stories boldly in prayer gatherings, group settings, or even personal conversations stirs faith in others and triggers God's hand to work again in your life and those around you. Testimonies strengthen the faith of the community and serve as a prophetic declaration: God is still enthroned and actively working on behalf of His people.

To make the most impact, write down your testimonies regularly. Keep a journal of God's good deeds, and revisit it often, especially during times of discouragement. When you declare these victories with conviction, you become a mouthpiece for divine power. It's as if you're inserting fuel into the fire of faith, igniting fresh hope and expectancy in your heart and in the hearts of others. Never diminish the significance of your story—every detail, every miracle, every act of God's mercy contributes to His greater glory. Use your testimony as a weapon in warfare, a shield in times of doubt, and an offering of praise, knowing that every declaration glorifies the King of kings and reminds the enemy that God's power is undefeated.

Living with humility and gratitude shapes a life of worship that continually honors God's sovereignty. When setbacks, pain, or deception threaten to define your story, choosing humility keeps your heart anchored in God's truth, recognizing that all good things come from Him. Gratitude, on the other hand, shifts focus from what was lost or what remains to the countless blessings already received. This posture of thankfulness refocuses your heart, reminding you that God's grace is sufficient and His mercy endures forever. It is in humility that you acknowledge your dependence on Him, opening your spirit for divine intervention and favor. Gratitude propels you beyond superficial thankfulness; it becomes a way of life—an authentic recognition that nothing escapes God's notice, and everything supernatural begins with a thankful spirit.

Practicing humility and gratitude daily can be as simple as starting each morning with a prayer that acknowledges God's sovereignty and giving thanks for His many blessings, big and small. When difficulties arise, maintaining this attitude becomes even more vital. Instead of questioning or complaining, you reaffirm God's goodness, trusting that His plan is perfect even when life's circumstances are trying. This lifestyle transforms worship from a scheduled activity into an ongoing attitude. It influences how you speak, how you respond to setbacks, and how you engage with others. A humble heart recognizes the need for God's grace, and a grateful heart acknowledges His divine hand in every detail of life. Together, humility and gratitude become a shield against pride and despair, anchoring you firmly in worship that honors God's majesty and sovereignty.

Remember, genuine humility allows you to receive God's love without resistance, and gratitude opens the door for increased blessings. Cultivate these qualities intentionally by reflecting on God's faithfulness daily and sharing gratitude openly with others.

As you do, you become a living testament that God's glory is best revealed in lives surrendered in humility and overflowing with thankfulness. This kind of worship doesn't depend on circumstances but is rooted deep within your spirit, honoring God regardless of what battles you face. When your heart remains humble and grateful, His presence becomes more tangible, His power more evident, and your life more deliberately aligned with His divine purposes, constantly giving Him the recognition He deserves as the source of every victory.

12. RECLAIMING YOUR DESTINY AND PURPOSE

Rediscovering God's Call for Your Life

Understanding God's purpose for your life begins with a deliberate pursuit of His presence. When life has left you feeling hurt, broken, or deceived, it can be challenging to hear His voice clearly. Yet, it is in moments of quiet intimacy—when you intentionally slow down and open your heart—that God's divine plan starts to unfold. Prayer becomes more than just speaking; it transforms into listening. Setting aside time each day to seek His face, away from distractions, allows you to tune your spirit to the Holy Spirit's gentle whisper. Remember, seeking God isn't a one-time act but a daily discipline that deepens your relationship with Him. As you do so, open your Bible and read with expectancy, asking Him to reveal His specific purpose for your season. God's purpose is often revealed through His Word, through circumstances, and through divine encounters, but only when your heart is attuned to His voice. This is not about striving to find answers through your own strength but surrendering and trusting that as you seek, God's clarity will more clearly emerge, guiding you through every hurt and setback.

As you press into God, you begin to understand that His purpose for your life is more than just a general calling; it is specifically tailored for your season. Clarity often comes through prayer, meditation on scripture, and moments of genuine stillness before Him. During these times, God often reveals His plans gradually, like a gentle whisper that needs attentive ears. Practical steps include journaling your thoughts and impressions during prayer, listening for patterns in scripture, or noting recurring words and themes that stand out. Sometimes, God allows circumstances that seem difficult or confusing to draw attention to a particular purpose. Trust that His ways are higher than yours, and His purpose is rooted in love, redemption, and abundance. Remember, seeking His face is an act of love—no different than pursuing a close friendship—and it is in that pursuit that your heart is aligned to what He desires for this season of your life.

Once you have begun to grasp God's purpose for your current season, the next step is aligning your goals with His kingdom plans. This alignment isn't about fitting God's purpose into your personal agenda but transforming your goals to reflect His sovereign will. It requires humility and surrender, acknowledging that God's plans are greater than yours and that your life is ultimately for His glory. To begin this process, evaluate your desires and ambitions through the lens of Scripture, asking if they serve His kingdom or if they place your comfort above His calling. Prayer remains vital here, as it guides your decisions and confirms whether your goals are aligned with God's heart. This process often involves surrendering some of your personal aspirations that may be good, but not what God intends for your season. Consider asking God for wisdom and divine direction before making key decisions, trusting that He will redirect your paths toward purpose and fulfillment.

Aligning goals with God's plans also involves practical steps such as setting intentions that serve others, participating in community or ministry that reflects His love, and engaging in acts of obedience that reinforce His kingdom work. Reflect on the gifts, talents, and resources God has placed within you, recognizing they are tools for fulfilling His purpose. For example, if you discover your calling is tied to encouraging others, look for ways to serve through mentoring, speaking, or supporting those hurt by life's setbacks. Remember, aligning your goals isn't a one-time event, but a continuous process of checking your motives and adjusting as you grow in understanding and obedience. By prayerfully partnering with God in this way, your pursuits become a part of a larger divine narrative, ensuring that every effort contributes to His kingdom's expansion and His plan for your life's destiny.

Ultimately, aligning your goals with His plans brings a sense of peace, purpose, and empowerment. It shifts your focus from self-centered ambitions to kingdom-centered pursuits, revealing that your life has eternal significance. As you continually surrender your desires and seek His direction, you'll find that your efforts are more fruitful and impactful, bringing not just personal fulfillment but also eternal rewards. Trust that God's blueprint for your life is perfect, and as you commit to this alignment, you'll step into a destiny that fully reflects His glory and purpose for your season. Walking in this alignment also means remaining flexible, ready to pivot or change direction as God reveals new insights, always anchored in the truth that His plans are good, loving, and worth pursuing above all else.

We serve a God of reversal. A God who redeems, restores, and repays. When the enemy invades, God always makes a way to bring His people out—stronger, richer, wiser, and walking in multiplied favor.

Look at Job

Look at Joseph.

Look at Naomi.

Look at YOU.

You were never forgotten. You were being *positioned.*

From **betrayal, envy, emotional pain, ungratefulness, deceit to spiritual grounding, vindication, and triumphant promotion,** centered around a **true-to-life story**, grounded in **Scripture**, and built for **healing, inspiration, and fire-filled restoration**.

There's Something Your Spirit Already Knows.

You didn't just stumble into warfare. You didn't just experience loss. The chaos wasn't random. The pain wasn't meaningless. What you went through—what tried to destroy you—was part of a **strategic demonic assignment** against your destiny.

But hear this clearly:

You survived it because you were chosen to reverse it.

Your heartbreak wasn't the end. Your betrayal wasn't the bottom. That financial hit, that emotional trauma, that spiritual drought—it wasn't punishment. It was preparation.

You've been delayed, distracted, and devoured. But now, **God is declaring a divine reversal over your life!**

This is more than a comeback.

This is not simply recovery.

This is repayment with interest.

"The LORD recompense thy work, and a full reward be given thee of the LORD God of Israel…" – Ruth 2:12

Heaven has calculated what the enemy stole—and now, **Heaven is releasing recompense.** It's time to *take it back*.

The enemy thought he buried you, but he didn't know you were a seed.

"And we know that in all things God works for the good of those who love Him…" – Romans 8:28

Let This Be Your Declaration:

"This is my season of GET BACK. I'm stepping over the line of loss and into the promise of divine repayment."

Take this moment and activate your **victory plan**:

Declare out loud:

This line is my recovery. I'm crossing over!

Because YOU are spiritually. Emotionally. Financially. **Prophetically aligned.**

The enemy must pay for what he stole.

God is commanding a **Take It Back Blessing** to overtake you.

GET BACK ACTIVATION

This isn't emotionalism—it's spiritual law.

Absolutely — and that's a powerful distinction.

When you declare, **"This isn't emotionalism—it's spiritual law,"** you're drawing a line between temporary feelings and eternal truth. This is about **activating Heaven's legal system** through faith, obedience, and prophetic instruction.

Let's break that down spiritually:

- **Emotionalism** moves you based on how you *feel*.
- **Spiritual law** moves Heaven based on what is *written*.

"Forever, O Lord, Your word is settled in Heaven." – Psalm 119:89

That means what you're declaring isn't hype — it's **Heaven's protocol**. The enemy must comply, not because you're loud, but because God's Word is **legally binding** in the courts of Heaven.

"This isn't emotionalism—it's spiritual law.

Heaven operates by decrees, not feelings.

When God says 'I will restore,' that's not a suggestion—it's a signed covenant.

Your obedience becomes your legal access point.

And your declaration?

It's your *courtroom statement* that forces the enemy to release what's yours."

Overcoming Past Failures and Setbacks

When life hits us hard with failure or disappointment, it's easy to see these moments as the end of the road. But spiritual growth teaches us differently: setbacks aren't final, they are simply setups for a greater comeback. God often uses our failures to shape and refine us, turning our pain into purpose. Every stumble, every disappointment, carries a lesson meant to deepen our character and strengthen our faith. It's vital to remember that what seems like defeat is often the foundation for a divine reset. Trust that behind every setback, there's a purpose working itself out, even if we cannot see it in the present moment. Instead of dwelling on what went wrong, shift your perspective and ask God to reveal what He's teaching you through this season of struggle. It is through these moments of brokenness that God often molds us into better versions of ourselves. Reflecting on past failures with humility and eyes of faith can help us see His guiding hand at work, gently steering us toward His divine destiny. Each time we respond to setbacks with faith, we learn resilience, and our testimony becomes a powerful witness to others who are also hurting. Remember, setbacks are not signs of abandonment, but signs of divine preparation for the next phase of your journey. Embrace them as opportunities to grow stronger, wiser, and more connected to God's plans for your life. The enemy may try to use failures to discourage, but God intends to use them to prepare you for greater victories.

God's word reassures us that even in moments of failure, His love remains constant. In 2 Corinthians 12:9, Paul speaks of God's grace being sufficient and His power perfected in weakness. This means that our weakness actually opens the door for God's strength to shine through in our lives. Rather than rushing to cover up our failures or feeling shame, we are encouraged to bring them before God, ask for His forgiveness, and learn from them. Through honest acknowledgment, we can see each setback as a lesson, a form of discipline, or even a corrective measure that guides us back onto His path. Maintaining a mindset of learning instead of losing encourages continuous growth. When we do this, we position ourselves to witness God's hand turning obstacles into opportunities, pain into praise, and setbacks into setups for extraordinary plans. The process involves forgiving yourself and trusting that God's mercy redeems every mistake, turning our past into a solid foundation for future success. What was meant for harm, God uses for good — this truth is meant to be a declaration we stand on, especially in seasons where failure presses heavily on our spirits. Every lesson carries a seed of divine wisdom, and when we plant these seeds in faith, we allow God's purposes to flourish in ways we never imagined.

One of the most powerful acts a believer can do in the face of brokenness is to speak God's promises over their life. Declaring God's faithfulness is a proactive step that shifts focus from fear and doubt to hope and trust. The enemy wants us to believe that our past failures define our future, but God's word reminds us that He is a master storyteller, rewriting even the most shattered narratives into beautiful testimonies of redemption. When we openly declare God's faithfulness, we assert our confidence that He is in control and that His plans for us are good. Proverbs 3:5-6 encourages us to trust in the Lord with all our heart and acknowledge Him in all our ways, knowing He will direct our steps. As we declare His faithfulness, we align ourselves with His promises, speaking life into dead situations and declaring that our future is secure in His hands. This act of faith is not just words; it is an affirmation that we believe God's plan is greater than any failure we've encountered. For example, if you have experienced loss, you can declare, "God is restoring what was lost, and He will bring beauty from ashes." Over time, these declarations become spiritual weapons, strengthening our faith and dismantling the enemy's lies. Repeating God's truth daily is crucial, especially when doubt tries to creep in, because speaking God's promises releases divine power and stirs the atmosphere for breakthrough.

Restoration is a recurring theme in Scripture. God is described as a God who restores the years the locusts have eaten (Joel 2:25). This means no matter how long you've endured setbacks or how much you feel broken, God specializes in making all things new. As you declare His faithfulness, you activate divine authority in your life. Remember, your words carry weight in the spiritual realm; through declaration, you create a spiritual environment where God's promises can manifest. Faith-filled declarations are often paired with prayer and action, creating a powerful combination that paves the way for supernatural restoration. Trust that God's favor is upon you, and His promises are yes and amen. By speaking life over your future, you actively participate in shaping your destiny, knowing that God is the ultimate author of your story. Keep declaring His faithfulness, not just as an affirmation, but as a personal proclamation of hope and victory. His promises are timeless, His faithfulness unchanging, and His desire for you is to walk in abundant restoration and renewed hope.

Stepping Into God's Greater Plan

Stepping into God's greater plan often begins with a conscious choice to move beyond comfort zones and embrace what He places before us. Many believers find themselves hesitant or uncertain when new doors open, especially after experiencing setbacks or pain. Yet, God's assignments are uniquely tailored to strengthen, refine, and prepare us for the purpose He has designed. To move forward boldly, we must first silence the voice of fear and doubt that often whispers, You're not ready or This is too much. Recognizing that God has called us to walk by faith, not by sight, is crucial. He equips those He calls, yet it requires a deliberate act of trusting Him enough to step in faith. When you decide to accept divine assignments, you are aligning yourself with His divine purpose, which is sometimes different from your personal agenda but always for your good.

Many women who have faced loss or disappointment suddenly find God opening new paths that seem unfamiliar or stretch their capacity. These moments are opportunities to rise in faith and say yes to the divine plans, even when they don't fully make sense. Remember, every assignment from God is an invitation to grow, to serve, and to reveal His glory through your life. Sometimes, stepping into these opportunities might mean taking a risk, forgiving someone who hurt you, or stepping into a new leadership role. The key is to trust that God's timing and plan are perfect, even if it appears uncertain or daunting. By leaning into prayer, seeking counsel from wise believers, and anchoring your heart in God's promises, you position yourself to walk confidently into the assignments He sets before you.

When you reflect on biblical examples, such as Moses stepping into his divine purpose despite his fears or Esther approaching the king with courage, it underscores the call to be brave. These stories show that God's plans often require us to stand firm and act decisively. You might find that the opportunities God presents involve stretching your faith and breaking through personal barriers. This is where your inner resolve becomes critical—believing that God's power working in you is greater than any obstacle. Take small, intentional steps daily—whether in prayer, service, or speaking up—and watch how God begins to uncover new dimensions of your purpose. The more you obey His leading, the more clarity you'll gain about your divine mission, and fear will diminish as trust takes its place.

Trusting in God's plan is often the hardest part when you're facing loss or setbacks. It's natural to question whether your circumstances are part of His greater purpose or if He has forgotten you. Yet, faith insists that God's purpose for your life is still unfolding, even when you are hurting inside. Obedience becomes your anchor; it's the act of doing what God commands regardless of how you feel or what your surroundings look like. When you choose obedience, you align yourself with His divine timetable and His promises. Faith is not passive; it is an active trust that His plans are perfect, and He is working everything together for good. This unwavering confidence helps you move forward with hope, knowing that the process of your purpose unfolding is ultimately for His glory and your good.

Many women find reassurance in the scriptures where trust in God's divine timing was key. Abraham waiting years for the promise of a son, Joseph enduring betrayal and imprisonment, yet still rising to authority, and Ruth remaining loyal and trusting God through hardship—all serve as proof that God's unfolding purpose requires perseverance and unwavering trust. Obedience involves daily surrender—choosing to follow God's word, even when it's uncomfortable or uncertain. It includes seeking His guidance through prayer, listening to His voice, and complying with His nudge, no matter how small. Over time, as you continue to walk in obedience, you will sense the gentle confirmation that your purpose is maturing and taking shape. Remember, faith is the confidence that the unseen is already happening in the spiritual realm, and your consistent obedience helps it manifest in tangible ways.

Trust also involves releasing control and relinquishing the outcome to God. Sometimes, this means surrendering your plans and embracing His. It may involve standing firm in the face of opposition or disappointment because you believe that God's promise and purpose are still being revealed. Journaling your journey of obedience can help you see how God is working in your life, providing clarity and encouragement during times of uncertainty. With every act of obedience, your faith becomes stronger, and you position yourself to receive even greater divine opportunities. Remember that God's divine purpose is a process—one that unfolds gradually as you remain faithful, obedient, and trusting in His perfect timing.

Heaven Has a Strategy for Your Comeback

Breakthrough Doesn't Happen by Accident — It Happens by Alignment

Recovery in the Kingdom isn't passive. It doesn't come by just waiting or wishing — it comes by **divine alignment with prophetic instruction**. God is not the author of confusion, but of **order**, and where there is **prophetic order**, there is **supernatural recovery**.

"Believe in the LORD your God, so shall you be established; believe His prophets, so shall you prosper." – 2 Chronicles 20:20

If you've been crying out, "Lord, when will I recover what I've lost?" — God's answer is:

"Follow the protocol, and I will release the promise."

A Word for the Weary

You've prayed. You've fasted. You've warned. But there's a divine principle that must be applied next:

Recovery is not just about faith — it's about **prophetic obedience**.

The widow in 2 Kings 4 had oil, but it stayed in the jar until she followed prophetic instruction.

Naaman had healing waiting, but it stayed locked in his flesh until he obeyed the prophetic act of dipping seven times.

Peter had provisions waiting, but the coin stayed in the fish until he went **fishing at Jesus' word**.

RECOVERY IS ALWAYS TIED TO A PROPHETIC ACT.

PROTOCOL #1: ASK GOD FOR A RECOVERY WORD

"Shall I pursue? Shall I overtake?" – 1 Samuel 30:8

"Pursue. For you shall surely overtake them, and without fail recover all."

David didn't assume recovery was automatic — he **inquired of the Lord.**

Before you act, pause. Pray. Ask:

"Lord, what is my recovery instruction? What is the strategy? Who do I need to disconnect from? Where should I re-sow? What should I reclaim?"

The enemy works through confusion, but **God restores through clarity**.

PROTOCOL #2: BREAK AGREEMENT WITH LOSS

As long as you identify with loss, you stay locked in it.

"Death and life are in the power of the tongue…" – Proverbs 18:21

Start declaring:

- "I am not broken — I am blessed."
- "I am not in delay — I am in divine transition."
- "I am not in poverty — I am in prophetic positioning."

Don't protect what God is trying to remove.

PROTOCOL #3: MOVE IN FAITH-FILLED ACTION

Faith without works is dead. That means recovery requires **motion**.

- The lepers were healed **as they went.** (Luke 17:14)
- The Red Sea parted **after Moses lifted the rod.** (Exodus 14:16)
- Provision came for the widow **after she poured.** (2 Kings 4:5)

What prophetic action is God asking of you?

Sow again.

Call again.

Apply again.

Write again.

Forgive again.

Build again.

Your miracle is often on the other side of your movement.

Protocol #4: Sow Where You Want to Go

"Those who sow in tears will reap with shouts of joy." – Psalm 126:5

Every harvest begins with a seed. Not out of obligation, but out of **expectation**.

A **Get Back Seed** is not just financial — it's **positional**. It says:

"I'm placing a demand on Heaven. I believe the Word. I am prophetically activating my future."

Even Isaac, during a famine, **sowed in the land**, and in the same year, reaped **a hundredfold.** (Genesis 26:12)

Protocol #5: Guard Your Gate

Recovery can't happen if the wound is still open.

You must **protect your atmosphere**.

"Above all else, guard your heart, for everything you do flows from it." – Proverbs 4:23

✓ Disconnect from toxic voices

✓ Set boundaries for healing

✓ Consume prophetic worship and the Word

✓ Surround yourself with *builders*, not *blamers*

✓ Write what God says — not what your emotions scream

You can't recover what you're still entertaining in destruction.

Real-Life Testimony: How Lisa Reclaimed Her Family

Lisa had been praying for the restoration of her family for over 12 years. Her marriage had ended. Her children were distant. Bitterness had crept in.

She asked God: "Why haven't I recovered what I lost?"

The Lord showed her: she never asked for **prophetic instructions.** She only asked for results.

She fasted for 3 days and received a specific word:

"Write them a letter. Release the offense. And sow a seed in faith for family restoration."

She obeyed, trembling. Within 30 days, one of her estranged sons reached out. Then another. Her ex-husband, after years of silence, began attending church again and reached out to apologize.

Her obedience **activated Heaven's hand.**

Your Prophetic Recovery Checklist

✓**Inquire of the Lord**

✓**Break the agreement with loss**

✓**Move in action**

✓**Sow in faith**

✓**Guard your gates**

Declare This Boldly:

"I will recover all.

I am aligned with Heaven's order.

I hear the instructions of the Lord, and I obey without hesitation.

I reject delay, disorder, and doubt.

My recovery is not a maybe — it's a matter of divine law.

I shall recover… with interest, with clarity, with power, and with joy!"

FINAL WORD

Beloved, God is not ignoring your pain.

He's aligning your path.

And if you follow the **prophetic protocol**, you will walk into **supernatural recovery** — faster than you think, greater than you dreamed, and **stronger than you've ever been**.

Your loss was real.

But your **get-back** is unstoppable.

13. BUILDING A SUPPORT SYSTEM OF FAITH AND ENCOURAGEMENT

Connecting with Like-minded Believers

Building genuine relationships with women and believers who align with your faith and mission is a powerful step towards spiritual growth and recovery. When you connect with others who share your convictions, it becomes easier to stay anchored in God's truth and maintain your focus amidst life's challenges. Fellowship isn't just about casual friendship; it's about intentionally surrounding yourself with those who will encourage your walk, hold you accountable, and pray with you during times of doubt or pain. By seeking out these connections, you create a support system rooted in shared values and divine purpose, which can serve as a shield against discouragement and deception.

In practical terms, this means actively participating in faith-based communities — whether through church groups, prayer circles, or Christian women's ministries — where authentic bonds can develop. It also involves being proactive in identifying women who are committed to walking the same path, those who desire to see you thrive, and who will speak truth and life into your situation.

Remember, such relationships often require effort and vulnerability, but the encouragement and strength gained are well worth it. When you align yourself with like-minded believers, God often uses those relationships to reinforce your faith and propel you toward your divine purpose, especially in seasons of brokenness or loss.

Looking for these connections should be intentional and prayerful. Ask the Holy Spirit to guide you toward women who will uplift and challenge you in truth. Attend prayer meetings, women's Bible studies, or mentorship groups with openness and a humble heart. As you develop these relationships, remain transparent about your struggles, knowing that authenticity invites divine healing and mutual support. Remember, God designed believers to be part of a body, and with each new relationship, you strengthen your spiritual resilience, enabling you to stand firm in the face of warfare, hurt, and deception.

Once you've begun establishing fellowship with like-minded believers, the next crucial step is to cultivate an environment of encouragement and accountability. This isn't about superficial positivity but about genuine, scripture-rooted edification that lifts your spirit and sharpens your faith. Encouragement serves as a buoy when you're sinking under the weight of grief or setbacks, reminding you of God's promises and His sovereignty over every situation. Spiritual accountability, on the other hand, is about having trustworthy friends who ask the tough questions, pray with you, and hold your feet to the fire when you drift or lose sight of God's truth.

Creating a cycle of mutual encouragement means sharing your victories and vulnerabilities openly, without shame or fear of condemnation. It's about trusting others to speak life into your circumstances and to gently confront any area where you may be compromising or wandering away from God's purpose for your life. Accountability partners can help you recognize stagnation or wrong mindsets that hinder your healing process. They serve as a mirror, reflecting Christ's love and truth even when it's uncomfortable, reminding you of your identity in Christ and your divine calling.

It's helpful to establish clear boundaries and expectations in these relationships so that encouragement remains honest and biblically grounded. Regular prayer sessions and honest conversations about your progress, setbacks, and temptations can become lifelines that prevent you from falling back into despair or deception. Remember, God often uses community to refine us and to deposit His strength in our spirits. When you surround yourself with believers who are committed to walking alongside you, you gain not only emotional comfort but also spiritual protection, which is essential in spiritual warfare, healing from hurt, and overcoming deception.

Developing such relationships also involves being intentional about investing in others' lives. As you give encouragement and accountability, you will discover that your faith grows stronger, and a sense of purpose begins to emerge from your shared journey. Prayer partnerships and accountability circles can become your armor in moments of weakness, reminding you that you are never alone in this walk. Trust in God's timing; often, the most impactful relationships develop over time, and as they do, they will serve as anchors, pulling you closer to His divine plan for your life.

Finally, remember that seeking out fellowship and accountability is an ongoing process. It requires humility, consistency, and a heart open to divine correction and edification. When your focus remains on Christ and your desire to serve Him faithfully, God will connect you with the right people who will uplift, challenge, and equip you for the spiritual battles ahead. These relationships will not only redefine your journey of healing but also multiply your strength in faith, resilience, and hope, empowering you to walk boldly in your divine calling.

BETRAYED BUT NOT BROKEN.

GOD WILL USE WHAT CUTS YOU TO CROWN YOU

You Never Saw It Coming

She trusted them.

She gave more than loyalty — she gave access.

She loved without hesitation, invested without fear, and gave without limits.

But in the end, they walked away dragging your name, where your character never walks

. No explanation. No apology.

Just silence. Absence. And betrayal.

Whether it was the people you toiled for, a lover, friend, family, staff, close allies, church sisters and brothers, or even a spiritual leader, what cut the deepest was that **they knew you**, and still hurt you.

This wasn't an attack from an enemy.

It was **a Judas kiss** from someone you let in.

The Weight of Betrayal

Betrayal shatters more than trust.

It disrupts your identity.

It makes you question:

- Was I foolish?
- Did I mishear God?
- Am I not worthy of loyalty?

But listen closely:

Your betrayal wasn't your breaking. It was your birthing.

Jesus Understands Betrayal

You are not alone. Your Savior was betrayed, too.

- Judas sold Him for silver.
- Peter denied Him.
- His disciples scattered.
-
- And he still chose love.

"Even my close friend in whom I trusted, who ate my bread, has lifted his heel against me." – Psalm 41:9

Jesus didn't just die for you — He walked through betrayal to show you how to survive it.

If Jesus was betrayed and still fulfilled His destiny, so will you.

God Will Use What Cuts You to Crown You

Let's talk about Joseph.

- Betrayed by his brothers.
- Sold into slavery.
- Forgotten in prison.
- Lied on by Potiphar's wife.

But years later, standing in power, Joseph looked at the very ones who betrayed him and said:

"You meant evil against me, but God meant it for good…" – Genesis 50:20

Joseph didn't just recover — he ruled.

What was meant to bury him became the path to the palace.

PERSONAL STORY: KELL BETRAYAL BECAME HER BREAKTHROUGH

Kell, a 22-year-old business owner, decided to hire an older woman from her own community—someone she believed shared not just her nationality, but her values. The woman was helpful, wise, and quickly became more than just an employee. She offered guidance, helped make key decisions, and was included in meetings, plans, and even given access to client details and contracts. Together, they seemed to be building something solid, something lasting.

Until one day, the unthinkable happened.

Kell discovered that the woman she had trusted like a mentor had created her own receipt book, secretly collecting payments for services under the table. It soon came to light that she had registered a business with a nearly identical name, offering the exact same services… all while still employed by Kell. Funds were being quietly redirected. Clients were being poached. And her goal? To bring Kell's business to collapse, take over the space, and rehire the staff under her own brand.

The betrayal was devastating.

Worse than the financial blow was the emotional one. News spread that this had been premeditated—calculated deceit, planned out to destroy something Kell had poured her heart and soul into.

But God would not let it stand.

In an unexpected twist, news broke that the woman's husband had suddenly passed away. In the wake of that tragedy, everything unraveled. She lost the business she tried to build on deception, her credit was ruined, and she nearly lost her home.

But for Kell, the deepest loss wasn't money or momentum—it was trust. Trust in people. Trust in her ability to discern character. Trust in the idea that goodness is always returned with goodness.

One night, in the quiet aftermath of that storm, God whispered something that shifted everything:

"They broke your trust, but not your destiny."

That single sentence healed something deep. And Kell made a decision that night—not to pursue revenge, but to pursue **restoration**.

She chose grace over grudge.

Prayer over pettiness.

Alignment over anger.

And the reward?

Within months, a global opportunity opened—one that catapulted her far beyond the reach of local sabotage. She didn't fight back. She didn't campaign to clear her name. She let God be both **defender** and **promoter**.

"The stone the builders rejected has become the cornerstone." – Psalm 118:22

The very one they tried to replace became the one God elevated.

Not because she forced a comeback—

But because she surrendered to the betrayal and let God build something **no one could tear down.**

BETRAYAL IS A DOOR — NOT A DEATH SENTENCE

Don't confuse **removal** with **rejection**.

Sometimes God allows them to walk away so your **divine assignment** can walk in.

You're not broken — you're being **rebuilt**.

"After you have suffered a little while, He will restore, confirm, strengthen, and establish you." – 1 Peter 5:10

SIGNS THAT YOU'RE HEALING FROM BETRAYAL

1. You stop rehearsing the pain and start releasing the weight.
2. You realize you're not bitter — just wiser.
3. You can bless them and mean it, because they were necessary.
4. You stop needing the apology, because **you got the revelation**.

ACTIVATION TIME

"I was betrayed, but I am not broken.

I was wounded, but I am not worthless.

I am rising from this betrayal wiser, stronger, anointed, and unshaken.

What they meant to kill me — God is using to **crown me**."

ACTION: LET IT GO, SO YOU CAN GROW

"This betrayal is buried. My purpose is alive."

"God, I sow not in bitterness, but in boldness. I refuse to stay tied to the pain. I release them — and I **release myself** into the next level of glory."

ENCOURAGEMENT

Beloved, betrayal hurts — but it never has the final word.

The cross proves it.

Judas may have kissed you…

But God is about to **crown you**.

And when you rise from this? You won't even smell like smoke.

You've been betrayed… but you are NOT broken.

Accountability and Prayer Partners

Having prayer partners isn't just about asking for support; it is about forming a spiritual foundation rooted in unity and mutual accountability. When you align yourself with prayer warriors—those who stand fervently in faith—you create a safeguard that strengthens your battle against doubt, fear, and discouragement. These partners are the voices that remind you of God's promises and champion your spiritual growth, especially during times when your heart feels heavy or your hope wanes. Consistent prayer with trusted friends opens the door for divine strength to flow into your life, reminding you that you're never walking this journey alone. Their prayers serve as a shield, and their encouragement affirms your faith, helping you stay focused on God's sovereignty amid life's storms.

Choosing the right prayer partners involves more than just random connections; it requires discernment and a commitment to walk together in truth. Seek out those whose hearts align with God's word and whose lives reflect integrity and humility. Establish boundaries that honor your vulnerability, allowing space for honest conversations and transparent confession. Accountability in prayer partners extends beyond just agreeing to pray; it involves checking in regularly, sharing breakthroughs, and honestly confronting setbacks. When you invite someone into this sacred space, you are cultivating a relationship rooted in trust and mutual encouragement. This partnership becomes more than a prayer chain—it becomes a lifeline that bolsters your faith during seasons of struggle.

In practical terms, consider setting specific goals for your prayer partnership. Decide how often you'll connect, whether through prayer calls, text messages, or in person, and commit to honoring those times. Share your prayer requests openly and invite your partner to do the same, creating an environment of transparency. Remember, accountability isn't about perfection; it's about consistency and perseverance. Celebrate the victories—whether they are spiritual breakthroughs, restored hope, or answered prayers—and encourage each other to keep pressing forward. When you stay committed to these partnerships, you tap into divine power that can elevate your faith, helping you remain steadfast even when circumstances seem overwhelming. This mutual accountability can transform your prayer life into a powerhouse of hope and resilience.

Being honest about your journey—particularly your struggles, doubts, and setbacks—creates space for divine insight and encouragement. Vulnerability is a powerful tool in the life of a believer because it invites God's healing and guidance into areas of brokenness. As you share honestly with trusted friends or prayer partners, you open your heart to the divine truths that can bring clarity and reassurance. Sometimes, simply articulating your pain can lift a burden and allow God's peace to settle in. Furthermore, your transparency can inspire others to remain steadfast, knowing they are not alone in their battles. Sharing your journey also keeps you alert to God's movements in your life, helping you recognize divine signals and messages that might otherwise go unnoticed amid chaos or confusion.

When you share your experiences, be intentional about seeking divine insight. Pray for wisdom to interpret the situations you face and ask the Holy Spirit to reveal lessons hidden within your pain. Often, God uses seasons of hardship to refine our faith and produce fruit we never imagined. Journaling your journey can be a helpful way to track where God shows up, how He answers prayers, or helps you see circumstances from a new perspective. Additionally, listening for God's voice amid your sharing invites divine strategies and responses that can pivot your outlook toward hope. Remember, your testimony has the power to ignite faith in others, proving that God's grace is sufficient to carry us through life's most difficult moments. When you openly share your journey, you invite divine insight that leads to greater understanding and strengthened faith.

Another crucial aspect of sharing your journey involves creating space for others' testimonies as well. Listen actively and with compassion; this exchange cultivates a sense of community and unity among believers. As you witness God's work in others' lives, your faith is stirred, and you are reminded of His faithfulness. Maintain a posture of humility and gratitude, recognizing that every step of your journey is part of God's divine plan. This openness fosters accountability, encourages perseverance, and keeps your spiritual eyes fixed on the Lord's goodness. Ultimately, sharing your journey isn't just about revealing your story—it's about inviting God's divine insight to guide each step forward, unveiling new layers of strength, wisdom, and hope that empower you to keep walking in faith.

Leveraging Testimony for Empowerment

When you openly share what God has done in your life, it becomes a powerful tool to uplift others. Your testimony of victory over hardship, sickness, loss, or doubt demonstrates God's faithfulness in real, tangible ways. For women who are healing from pain or setbacks, recounting how God's grace brought them through can ignite hope in others still fighting their battles. Sharing these stories not only affirms your own faith but also builds a sense of community where everyone recognizes they are not alone in their struggles. Stories of breakthroughs become a foundation upon which others can stand, reminding everyone that God's power is still active and willing to intervene on their behalf.

As you share your victories, focus on authenticity. Be transparent about the struggles you faced, but also emphasize God's strength that carried you through. This honesty fosters vulnerability and trust, encouraging others to open up about their own issues. When women hear real stories of overcoming fear, discouragement, or deception, it helps them see that their setbacks are not the end, but a setup for God's glory to be revealed. Your testimony can serve as a rallying cry within your faith group, pushing others to believe again—believe in healing, restoration, and the unchanging goodness of God. Remember, testimonies are a conduit for divine encouragement and are often the missing puzzle piece in someone's journey to victory.

Encourage other women to share their stories, too. Sometimes, a simple question like "Has God brought you through something recently?" can open the door for someone to reveal God's hand at work in their life. Creating a safe space for these testimonies fosters unity and mutual empowerment. As women witness each other's victories, their faith is fortified, and they are reminded that God's promises are still active today. Never underestimate the ripple effect of your story; it can ignite a wildfire of faith that spreads beyond your immediate circle, touching lives in ways you may never fully see. Your victories are more than personal triumphs—they are seeds of hope in the spiritual soil of your community.

In the spiritual battles that many women face—whether against brokenness, deception, or discouragement—your testimony becomes a declaration of God's sovereignty. When you speak of

God's goodness in your life, you are effectively wielding it as a weapon to counteract negative voices or lies rooted in defeat. Every story of God's intervention is a powerful proclamation over every lie of the enemy, reminding heaven and earth that God's power is greater than any obstacle. Declaring your testimony out loud, especially in prayer or during spiritual warfare, releases faith into the atmosphere and activates divine intervention. It is a way to reinforce the truth that God's promises and power are active in your daily life.

Think of your testimony as a shield in spiritual warfare—a declaration that God's power is more than enough to break every chain of doubt, fear, or deception. When you recount what God has done openly, it shifts the spiritual atmosphere from one of defeat to victory. For women fighting internal battles, the act of proclaiming God's goodness becomes a bold statement of faith that God is still working miracles. These declarations also serve as a reminder that our words are not empty; they are rooted in truth and backed by God's power. Declaring your testimony loudly and confidently can inspire others to do the same, turning their faith into a rallying cry that awakens the divine power within them.

Use scripture to reinforce your declarations. For instance, referencing verses like Psalm 34:8, Oh, taste and see that the Lord is good, or Revelation 12:11, which speaks of overcoming through the blood of the Lamb and the word of your testimony, gives biblical authority to your words. When women stand on God's word and declare what He has done, they become active participants in spiritual warfare, resisting the enemy's tactics and asserting God's victory. Remember, your testimony isn't just a story; it's a strategic declaration of God's ongoing sovereignty and goodness. Speak it with authority, and watch how it shifts the spiritual atmosphere around you and those you are called to serve.

14. MAINTAINING VICTORY THROUGH WORSHIP AND PRAYER

Worship as Warfare

Worship is more than mere songs or routines; it is a powerful weapon that can transform the atmosphere around us. When believers engage in sincere worship, it invites God's presence to fill the environment, pushing back darkness and oppressive spirits. Scripturally, we see this demonstrated in 2 Chronicles 20, where King Jehoshaphat and the people of Judah faced a vast army. Instead of relying solely on weapons or strategic plans, they chose to worship, sending singers ahead of the army, singing praises to God. The result was a divine surge of power that confused the enemy and led to their victory. This example reveals that worship has the extraordinary ability to carry divine authority into any space, turning spiritual battles into victories. As worshipers, we become catalysts, releasing God's power through heartfelt declarations and praise, shifting the unseen realms where battles truly take place.

To harness this power effectively, believers should recognize that worship is not just a response but a strategic approach. When confronting spiritual opposition or personal setbacks, worship becomes an act of spiritual warfare. Begin by openly declaring God's sovereignty, His promises, and His authority in your life. Worship invites divine power to move on your behalf, breaking strongholds and dismantling the works of darkness. Remember, the atmosphere responds to authentic praise; it is not about performance but about positioning your heart in humility and faith. As Psalm 22:3 states, "God inhabits the praises of His people." When you lift your voice in worship, you make space for His presence to settle, His power to manifest, and His victory to unfold. Worship acts as a spiritual clearest signal that heaven is open and that divine assistance is active in your circumstances.

In times of trouble or adversity, it can be tempting to rush into problem-solving or to let fear and frustration dominate our thoughts. Yet, the biblical pattern shows that worship should be our initial response. When Daniel faced the lion's den, or when Paul and Silas found themselves imprisoned, their first instinct was to worship, lifting praise to God despite the internal or external chaos. By choosing worship first, we align ourselves with God's power rather than our limitations. Worship redirects our focus from the problem to the Provider, transforming anxiety into faith and despair into hope. This shift in attitude is crucial because it unlocks divine intervention and causes the enemy's tactics to backfire. Remember, worship is not just a last resort but a strategic battlefield move that positions us to see God move swiftly and powerfully.

Practicing worship as your first response involves developing a habit of praising in every situation, whether through singing, declaring scriptures, or simple prayers of gratitude. When faced with setbacks, instead of dwelling on what went wrong, lift your voice in worship and thank God for His presence and His promises. This act of faith activates God's power and opens portals of heaven over your circumstances. It also builds spiritual resilience, making you less vulnerable to discouragement and more attuned to divine solutions. Over time, this practice rewires your response pattern so that worship naturally becomes your default when challenges arise. This not only shifts your own spiritual state but also influences the atmosphere around you, creating a ripple effect of divine activity that can impact your family, community, and even your church environment.

In practice, start your days with worship sessions, declare God's word aloud over your challenges, and incorporate praise into your prayer routines. When a crisis hits, resist the urge to panic or complain. Instead, take a moment to lift your voice, praising God for His goodness and sovereignty. This not only calms your spirit but also activates angels and divine resources that are always ready to respond to worship. Remember, your faith-filled praise can turn battles into victories and setbacks into setups for God's glory. As you train yourself to worship first and foremost, you will see more tangible evidence of God's power flowing through every challenge you encounter.

Consistent Prayer and Supplication

Creating a consistent prayer routine is essential for those seeking to stay connected with God amid life's challenges. Discipline in prayer is not about mechanical repetition but about cultivating a heart posture that continually seeks God's presence. When you make prayer a daily habit, it becomes the lens through which you interpret your circumstances and the anchor that keeps your soul grounded. Regular dialogue with God develops a sensitivity to His voice, making it easier to discern His will in every situation. This consistency builds spiritual strength, enabling you to stand firm against setbacks and the wounds of life. It's about waking up each day with a determined heart to seek God's face, knowing that through this communion, His guidance becomes clearer and His power more accessible.

Developing this disciplined prayer life requires intentionality, turning prayer from an occasional activity to a core part of your daily rhythm. Set aside specific times—perhaps morning, mealtime, or bedtime—where undistracted prayer becomes natural. Use scripture as your foundation; meditating on God's promises helps anchor your requests and align your heart with His will. Writing out your prayers or journaling can deepen your connection, making your communication with God more personalized and honest. Remember, consistency isn't about perfection but perseverance; some days you may feel more connected than others, but showing up day after day cultivates a spiritual discipline that ultimately shapes your mindset and strengthens your spirit. As you do so, you begin to see prayer as not just a request bucket but a transformative encounter that shapes your identity and purpose.

Persisting in prayer, even when answers seem delayed, is a powerful act of faith. Supplication isn't just about asking once; it's about staying steadfast, trusting that God hears every cry and that His timing is perfect. When you continue to pour out your heart before Him, you declare that your trust is rooted in His sovereignty, not in immediate results. This kind of perseverance positions you for divine breakthroughs, because God's timing often involves working behind the scenes, orchestrating things for your good in ways you might not understand immediately. Every time you persist, you are engaging in a spiritual war that shifts the atmosphere over your life, releasing God's power into situations that seem unchangeable. Remember, some breakthroughs require persistence in prayer—think of it as a spiritual battle where your relentless faith becomes the weapon that shifts the course of your circumstances.

Persistent supplication is not about obsessing over results but about cultivating a posture of unwavering trust. It means continuing to pray despite setbacks, doubts, or delays, knowing that God's promises are sure. Your consistent prayers serve as a divine summons, inviting heaven's intervention into earth's difficulties. Over time, this persistent effort weakens the enemy's grip and strengthens your faith muscle, empowering you to stand victorious in Christ. A practical step is to keep a prayer journal, noting your petitions and God's responses, which encourages you to see His hand at work. Be reminded that many biblical heroes, from Hannah to Daniel, exemplified persistence in prayer, and their breakthrough stories remind us that perseverance is often the key to unleashing God's greatest answers. Stand firm knowing your earnest prayer is not lost but stored in heaven, ready to manifest at the right moment.

Finally, remember that prayer is a tool for warfare, healing, and breakthroughs. It's not just about asking for things but about building a relationship that shifts spiritual realities. When you view your persistent prayers as a form of spiritual authority, it becomes easier to keep going even when results are not immediately seen. In times of doubt or discouragement, recall that God is working on your behalf, orchestrating circumstances for good. Maintaining focus and faith keeps your prayers alive, transforming ordinary petitions into divine declarations that influence the unseen forces. In this practice, you are not merely speaking into the air; you are engaging with the Creator of the universe, who responds to persistent faith. Keep pressing in, knowing that divine breakthroughs are often released through perseverance rooted in unwavering trust in God's power and love.

Staying Vigilant Spiritually

Staying vigilant in the Spirit requires an active awareness of the unseen battles happening around and within us. Spiritual attacks often come subtly, disguised as doubts, confusion, or sudden feelings of despair that overwhelm our hearts. Recognizing the signs of these assaults is crucial because they're designed to weaken our faith, derail our purpose, and cause us to doubt God's goodness. Discernment becomes a spiritual muscle that must be exercised daily, questioning thoughts, motives, and situations to see if they align with God's truth. Prayer becomes a vital tool in this process, acting as a spiritual radar that reveals whether an attack is in progress or if divine intervention is at hand. Often, divine breakthroughs come when we remain sensitive to the Holy Spirit's whispers, catching glimpses of God's hand moving in the midst of chaos or confusion. When we develop a habit of alertness, we position ourselves to not only defend our spirit but also to catch divine opportunities for breakthroughs that can restore hope or shift circumstances for good. The key is to stay rooted in God's Word and to cultivate a lifestyle of listening—asking Him daily to reveal what is of Him and what is a deception or distraction meant to throw us off course.

Being spiritually alert isn't about paranoia or living in fear but about a confident awareness grounded in scripture. The Bible reminds us in 2 Corinthians 10:4-5 that the weapons of our warfare are not carnal but mighty through God to pull down strongholds, including every high thing that exalts itself against the knowledge of God. When attacks come, they often catch us off guard because we aren't paying attention; thus, staying watchful helps us catch these schemes early. It's about learning to discern when negative thoughts are from the enemy or when circumstances are trying to manipulate our faith and peace. Opportunities for divine intervention often look like sudden bursts of peace, clarity, or a scripture that drops into our spirit exactly when we need it. When we keep our eyes open spiritually, we begin to see these God moments more clearly—be they a divine connection, unexpected provision, or peaceful reassurance amid turmoil. Cultivating this awareness grows as we consistently seek God through prayer, worship, and the study of His Word, tuning our spiritual ears to His voice amidst the noise of life.

Guarding your heart and mind is not a one-time act but a continuous discipline rooted in intimacy with God. The enemy aims to infiltrate our thoughts and emotions, planting seeds of doubt, fear, or discouragement that can take root and produce destruction in our spirit. Prayer acts as a spiritual shield, a direct line of communication that keeps our hearts close to God's heart and those negative influences at bay. Praising and worshiping Him daily refocuses our gaze on His sovereignty and goodness, dispelling lies that seek to distort our perception of His promises. When we fill ourselves with praise, we activate heaven's atmosphere, which pushes back against darkness and confusion. This ongoing practice cultivates a resilient spirit that refuses to be swayed by circumstances or negative thoughts. Instead, it anchors us in truth, reminding us of God's unwavering love and faithfulness. Scripture encourages us to meditate on His Word day and night, making it a weapon against every lie the enemy tries to whisper. Psalms and songs of praise aren't just moments of worship; they become declarations over our lives, demolishing fear and establishing peace as the default state of our hearts.

Developing a daily rhythm of prayer and praise builds a fortress around your mind—a mental and emotional sanctuary that protects you from harmful influences. When you start your day with intentional moments of worship, you're asserting your authority over the enemy and choosing to walk with a heart prepared for fight or flight. It's empowering to declare God's Word over your situation, speaking life to your circumstances rather than letting fear or anxiety run unchecked. Practical steps include setting a specific time each day for prayer, playing worship music to shift your atmosphere, or journaling scriptures that speak to your current challenges. The discipline of consistently worshiping transforms how you respond to setbacks by anchoring your soul in God's truth. Over time, this not only shields you from spiritual attacks but also awakens your spiritual senses to divine encounters, revelations, and interventions that might otherwise go unnoticed. Remember, victory often begins in the secret place, where prayer and worship are the anchors of your victory in Christ.

15. WALKING IN CONTINUAL VICTORY AND FAITH

Developing a Lifestyle of Declaration

Engaging in daily faith declarations is like planting seeds of hope and strength within your spirit. When you commit to speaking God's promises over your life each day, you are actively aligning your mind and heart with His truth. These declarations serve as a spiritual armor, reminding you of the victory already won through Christ. Consistency is key; the more you declare God's Word, the more it becomes rooted deeply in your heart, shaping your mindset and overcoming doubt or despair that may try to creep in from past wounds or setbacks. Over time, this practice rewires your thinking, leading to a renewed perspective that affirms your identity in Christ and His power working through you.

Start by creating simple, powerful declarations rooted in Scripture. For instance, speaking aloud, I am more than a conqueror through Christ who loves me, or God supplies all my needs according to His riches in glory, which reinforces your faith daily. Make it a non-negotiable part of your routine—whether during your morning quiet time, driving in your car, or before you sleep.

Writing these declarations on sticky notes and placing them where you'll see them regularly helps to keep your mind focused on God's truth. The act of speaking out loud is important because it activates your faith and breaks the power of negative thoughts. Persisting in this practice eventually shifts your inner dialogue from defeat to victory, transforming how you see every challenge you face.

As you develop this daily habit, remember that faith declarations are not just words—they are spiritual weapons. They serve as reminders of God's promises to heal, restore, and give you a future filled with hope. Using declarations rooted in Scripture creates a foundation of truth that cannot be shaken by circumstances. Consistent declaration builds a divine momentum, empowering you to stand firm even when circumstances scream otherwise. Over time, you'll notice a shift in your confidence, a deeper trust in God's word, and a heightened awareness of His presence guiding you through every season of life. Make your declarations personal, heartfelt, and rooted in God's promises, and watch how they begin to anchor your soul in victory rather than defeat.

Speaking life and God's promises over every area of your life is a declaration of faith that breaks the chains of despair and awakens hope. It's about actively choosing words that align with God's truth, even when your circumstances seem contrary. Your words have power; they create your reality. When you consistently declare God's promises—whether for healing, provision, relationships, or identity—you are inviting divine power to manifest in your life. This ongoing practice helps retrain your mind from a cycle of worry or hopelessness to one of faith and expectation. By speaking positive, hopeful words rooted in Scripture, you start to fill your environment with divine life, which impacts your atmosphere and the hearts of those around you.

For example, claim promises like, The Lord will restore what the locust has eaten, or I can do all things through Christ who strengthens me. These declarations become a shield against negative thoughts and words that can sometimes seep into your thinking through hurt or disappointment. Make it a habit to speak these over every area—your health, finances, family, emotional well-being, and spiritual growth. It's helpful to create a daily routine where you intentionally recite these promises, either aloud or silently, to reinforce your faith. When challenges arise, don't shy away from speaking God's Word over the situation—your words have authority, and speaking life invites heaven's intervention. Over time, this consistent declaration cultivates a hopeful mindset that becomes a source of strength during hard times.

Living out this practice reminds you that hope is a spiritual force, and your words are a key part of activating it. When you declare God's promises regularly, you are asserting your faith and positioning yourself for divine breakthroughs. It also encourages others around you to speak faith instead of fear, creating a community of hope-bearers. Remember, the seeds you plant today through your words will grow into the harvest of your tomorrow. Keep speaking life not just for yourself but for your household, your church, and your community, because faith activated through words has the power to transform lives. Focus on consistency and trust that as you declare God's truth, you are building a foundation from which victory flows naturally into every part of your life.

Avoiding Backsliding and Complacency

Spiritual complacency is a quiet danger that often lurks in the shadows when we least expect it. It's the subtle easing of effort, a moment when our hearts settle into a routine, and our fervor begins to fade without us realizing it. Many believers find themselves going through the motions, speaking words of faith without truly engaging their spirit or seeking God's presence with the urgency it deserves. This complacency robs us of the vitality needed for growth and leaves us vulnerable to backslide or lose momentum. The enemy loves it when believers become comfortable, because comfort breeds blindness to the areas where we need discipline and renewal.

Scriptural warnings remind us sternly about this danger. For instance, Revelation 3:15-16 exhorts believers to be vigilant, urging us to wake up from our spiritual slumber, for indifference makes us lukewarm and unfit for God's purpose. It's essential to recognize signs of complacency in our lives: a lack of prayer, neglecting the reading of His Word, or shrinking back when trials come instead of standing firm. Staying vigilant means actively checking our hearts, asking ourselves tough questions—are we still hungry for God's presence? Are our priorities aligned with His kingdom? Complacency can easily be disguised as peace or stability, but God wants us to continually press forward, not settle for comfort that diminishes our spiritual vitality.

To guard against sliding into complacency, we must intentionally cultivate disciplines that keep us alert. Regularly evaluating our walk with God, setting spiritual goals, and seeking accountability can prevent us from drifting. Remember, staying vigilant isn't about living in fear but about choosing to remain focused on Jesus and His calling. Faith requires intentional effort, like tending a garden. We must weed out the distractions and water ourselves daily with His Word and His Spirit. When danger signals arise—like apathy, discouragement, or drifting away—act promptly. Commit to renewing your urgency for God's work, and never allow the enemy to lull you into a false sense of security that dulls your spiritual senses.

The believer's journey is marked by seasons of renewal, where we intentionally reset our hearts back to God's purpose. Renewing your commitment involves more than just a superficial promise; it's a deliberate and heartfelt choice to reaffirm your desire to follow Christ wholeheartedly. Life's setbacks, losses, and disappointments can sometimes cause us to drift, making us question whether our faith still holds firm. Yet, in those moments, God calls us to reaffirm our vow—renew our vows of obedience, trust, and surrender. This act of renewal breathes fresh life into our spirits and restores the fire that may have cooled due to pain or discouragement.

Remaining engaged in active faith requires practical steps. First, reflect honestly on your current spiritual state. Are you thriving, or are you merely surviving? Ask God to reveal areas where complacency has taken root. Then, renew your commitment by setting tangible goals—whether it's increasing your prayer time, reading a chapter of Scripture daily, or serving others in love. Engaging actively also means staying connected to a community of believers who can motivate and correct us. Fellowship creates accountability and reminds us that we're not alone in this journey.

Furthermore, renew your passion through worship and gratitude. Praise God for what He has done while trusting Him for what He's yet to accomplish. Remember, faith is not static; it's an active pursuit. When you recommit, you're not only renewing vows to God but also fueling your own perseverance. Consistent engagement in spiritual disciplines—prayer, Scripture, fellowship, worship—cements your resolve and keeps the fire burning bright. Each act of commitment becomes a declaration that you choose to stand firm, even amid setbacks or failures. Trust that God's grace is sufficient to renew and restore, no matter how far you've fallen, and that each renewed step strengthens your overall spiritual health.

Practically, consider creating a renewal routine—perhaps a daily prayer of surrender, a weekly fast, or a journaling session to record God's faithfulness. These acts serve as reminders of your vows and help sustain your active faith. Remember, the goal is not perfection but perseverance. Keep your eyes fixed on Jesus, who is the author and perfecter of our faith. Each renewal is an encounter that refreshes your spirit and re-aligns your heart with God's purpose. Over time, this consistency builds resilience and prevents backsliding, allowing you to walk steadily in His grace, even through difficult seasons.

Living as a Conqueror in Christ

Understanding who you are in Christ is the first step toward living as a conqueror. Instead of seeing yourself as defeated or overwhelmed by life's challenges, begin to recognize your true identity rooted in Jesus. The Word constantly reminds us that in Him, we are more than conquerors and that victory has already been secured through His sacrifice and resurrection. This is not just a hopeful wish; it's a foundational truth to stand on each day. Whenever the enemy whispers doubt or reminds you of past failures, declare with confidence that you are loved, redeemed, and empowered by Jesus to overcome every obstacle.

Living as a victorious person isn't just a future hope—it's a present reality. You are called to see yourself through God's eyes, firmly established in Christ's victory. Speak out loud what the Word says about you. Phrases like "I am more than a conqueror," "I am forgiven," and "I am an overcomer" become daily declarations that reinforce your new identity. Faith is built when you consistently affirm what the Scriptures declare about you, and over time, these declarations become the lens through which you interpret every situation. Remember, your authority in Christ isn't based on feelings—it's rooted in truth that withstands circumstances and persists through every trial.

To deepen this perspective, you can remind yourself of personal testimonies of victory. Think about times when God delivered you from difficulty, healed you from sickness, or provided when resources seemed scarce. Each of these moments affirms your identity as a victorious child of God. The key is cultivating an unwavering confidence that your status as an overcomer is permanent, not temporary. This mindset transforms how you approach setbacks—they're simply opportunities to showcase God's power working through you to overcome. The more you declare your victory, the more you strengthen your spiritual muscles, making it easier to face life's battles with boldness and assurance.

Walking in divine authority means understanding that Christ has given you power over every area of your life—over fear, doubt, sickness, and discouragement. This authority is not something you earn; it is a gift from God through Jesus Christ. To walk confidently, you must first fully accept that God's promises belong to you and that His power resides within you through the Holy Spirit. Confidence doesn't come from your feelings but from aligning your mindset with God's Word. When you embrace your divine authority, you realize that you are authorized to speak life over situations and to command circumstances to line up with God's promises.

Living out this divine authority involves intentionality. It means speaking God's Word in faith, standing firm in prayer, and refusing to accept defeat as final. For example, if sickness tries to attack your body, declare scripture like Isaiah 53:5—By His stripes, I am healed. If fear attempts to creep in, remind yourself of 2 Timothy 1:7—God has not given me a spirit of fear, but of power, love, and a sound mind. Each declaration builds your confidence and reinforces your position as a ruler in Christ. Walking boldly also requires understanding that your authority isn't just about commanding others; it's about exercising spiritual dominion over negative mindsets, habits, and circumstances that oppose God's will for your life.

It's essential to recognize that this confidence is rooted in a relationship with Jesus. As you grow in intimacy with Him through prayer, study, and worship, your authority becomes more evident. You begin to operate less out of anxiety and more out of faith, knowing that the power of Christ works through you. Remember, every time you stand firm in your authority and declare God's promises, you are not just speaking words—you are activating heaven's resources and establishing God's kingdom principles on earth. This is a calling for every believer, especially those recovering from setbacks or hurting from past wounds, to step into the fullness of their divine inheritance—living as kings and queens in Christ, victorious in every area of life.

One practical tip is to create a personal declaration list based on scriptures that affirm your authority and victory. Repeat these declarations daily, especially during moments of prayer or when facing challenges. Over time, these words will become part of your spiritual DNA, empowering you to walk in confident authority, knowing that victory is already yours through Christ Jesus. As you do, you'll begin to see signs of that victory manifest in tangible ways—peace that surpasses understanding, breakthroughs in your circumstances, and a renewed sense of strength for every battle.

You Survived the War Because You Were Chosen for the Reward

You Didn't Just Come Through — You Came Out Crowned

This is not the end — it's the *release*.

You've read the truth.

You've cried through the loss.

You've shouted through the revelation.

And now, God says:

"The fight is finished. The reward is released."

Your story didn't end in trauma.

Your purpose wasn't buried in betrayal.

Your destiny wasn't destroyed by delay.

You made it.

And Heaven has been keeping record the entire time.

"For God is not unjust to forget your labor of love…" – Hebrews 6:10

What Is the Reward?

The reward isn't just stuff. It's not just houses, cars, or money.

The reward is…

✓Peace that makes no sense

✓Joy that cannot be shaken

✓Restoration that shocks your enemies

✓Honor where there was once humiliation

✓Divine acceleration in the place of delay

✓Legacy where there was once loss

✓*Presence* — not just blessings

And yes… **provision and prosperity too.**

"The LORD recompense thy work, and a full reward be given thee…" – Ruth 2:12

"If you are willing and obedient, you shall eat the good of the land." – Isaiah 1:19

♛ *You Didn't Lose — You Were Planted*

Seeds don't look like much when they're buried.

But now the soil has done its work.

The pain has broken.

The chains have fallen.

And the season of **fruitfulness** is here.

Everything that was taken…

Everything that was stolen…

Everything you cried over in secret…

Heaven is multiplying it openly.

DECLARATION: THE REWARD IS YOURS

Say this aloud with boldness:

"I have fought the good fight.

I have endured the storm.

I have passed the test.

And now, I step into my reward.

What the enemy took must now be returned, with interest.

I am not empty — I am full.

I am not broken — I am built.

I am not behind — I am right on time.

The reward is mine — and I receive it now in Jesus' name."

Instructions:

1. **Write Your "Get Back Manifesto"**
   - In your journal, list every area where God is rewarding you — spiritually, emotionally, financially, relationally. Call it your *"Get Back List."*

2. **Make Room for the Blessing**
   - Clean your physical space. Prepare. Expect. Honor the reward with **preparedness**.

Pray, "Lord, I'm not buying a blessing — I'm **honoring the covenant**. This seed closes the door on loss and opens the gate of **full reward**."

3. **Revisit This Book Every 30 Days**
   - This instruction is not a moment — it's a *movement*. Let these chapters keep cycling through your life.

YOUR JOURNEY HAS JUST BEGUN

You didn't read this book by accident.

You didn't endure the warfare without purpose.

You didn't cry those tears for nothing.

You are not who the enemy said you were.

You are **God's chosen vessel.**

You are **Heaven's proof that recovery is real.**

You are **the fulfillment of prophecy.**

Let this be your final word to the enemy and to yourself:

"Everything I lost, Heaven has restored.

What the enemy took, God has repaid.

And what was broken, God has rebuilt.

THE REWARD IS MINE."

FINAL BLESSING OVER YOU:

"I bless your hands to recover.

I bless your voice to prophesy.

I bless your feet to walk through open doors.

I bless your heart to trust again.

I bless your family, your finances, and your future.

May the God of recompense visit your life with undeniable favor.

May what took years be recovered in weeks.

And may you never forget — YOU GOT IT BACK."

What the Enemy Took!

Your tears were seeds.

Your faith was the key.

Your obedience was the trigger.

And now…

THE REWARD IS YOURS.

This is a prophetic season. You're not begging for a breakthrough—you're stepping into **a covenant promise** of recompense. Obey the word of God, and release your seed in faith, remember:

God is not mocked. What you sow in faith, you shall reap in victory.

The enemy took it—but Heaven is giving it back!

THE LAST TEARDROP AND THE RESCUE – VINDICATION AT LAST

There comes a moment in every believer's journey where pain meets purpose… where heartbreak meets Heaven… and where **what the enemy took is returned with fire**.

I have lived that moment.

This is not theory. This is my **true story** — written in blood, betrayal, and battle… but sealed in glory.

The Ones I Helped…

They sat at my table.

Ate from my hand.

Cried in my arms.

Held my trust.

I counseled them when no one else would.

I prayed them through hell.

I opened doors they couldn't reach.

I invested time, money, reputation — all in love.

And when could they stand on their own?

They **turned**.

With envy.

With lies.

With deception.

With calculated, barefaced betrayal that only a **Judas spirit** could understand.

Betrayal Is a Cross, Not a Curse

They didn't just turn on me — they tried to **tear down** everything God had built through me. My name. My ministry. My business. My character.

They whispered lies dressed in spiritual language.

They used scriptures to cover sabotage.

They twisted the truth until I didn't recognize myself in their stories.

And for a moment, I was tempted to retaliate.

To defend myself.

To clap back.

To expose them all.

But the Lord said:

*"Turn the other cheek — not in weakness, but in **warfare**."*

"The LORD will fight for you; you need only to be still." – *Exodus 14:14*

I Lied on the Floor in Tears — But I Got Up in Fire

The pain was so deep, I didn't just lose relationships — I nearly lost my **identity**.

There were nights when I cried until my body trembled — and I could feel the betrayal like cold steel in my back.

But in that place of silence… I met the **Spirit of Truth**.

He said:

"They lied to you…

They tried to bury you…

But I will **vindicate** you in front of every table that tried to remove your seat."

"Thou preparest a table before me in the presence of my enemies…" – *Psalm 23:5*

And suddenly… I wasn't crying anymore.

Suddenly… I didn't need their apology.

Suddenly… **my last teardrop hit the altar — and I rose in FIRE.**

Now the Fire Burns Within Me

I'm no longer trying to convince people who don't value my calling.

I'm no longer chasing platforms built on manipulation.

I'm no longer watering gardens that grow **jealousy**, not fruit.

Because now, the fire of God **burns in my belly**.

My roar has returned.

My voice has been restored.

And my **vindication is undeniable.**

Ungratefulness Is Worse Than Obeah

What they tried to curse… God has already covered.

Ungratefulness is a poison that breaks the covenant.

But **obedience breaks yokes**.

"No weapon formed against you shall prosper, and every tongue which rises against you in judgment, you shall condemn." – Isaiah 54:17

The witchcraft, the lies, the slander, the sabotage — none of it stood against **a woman anchored in the Word**.

Promotion Is Here — Not in Spite of the Fire, But Because of It

The very attacks that tried to bury me became the soil for my **promotion**.

- The same ones who lied now watch God lift me.
- The same ones who mocked now must witness the miracles.
- The same enemies who plotted now must bow to the outcome.

Just like Joseph, I can say:

"You meant it for evil, but God meant it for good." – Genesis 50:20

And like Hannah:

"Those who were full have hired themselves out for bread, but those who were hungry have ceased to hunger. The barren has borne seven..." – 1 Samuel 2:5

Final Prophetic Decree Over Your Life:

Say it loud, with boldness and tears if you must:

"The last tear I cried over betrayal was not in defeat — it was in transition.

I will never again cry over people God has removed.

I will never again bleed for those who feed off my pain.

I will never again shrink for comfort when God calls me to confront.

The reward is mine.

The fire is in me.

The anointing is heavier.

The vindication is sure.

I AM NOT WHO I WAS — I AM WHO GOD PROMISED.

What the enemy took…

Heaven returned with interest.

I forgive. I release. I rise."

This Is Not Just a Book — It's a Resurrection

To every woman who has been lied to…

To every leader who has been betrayed by the ones they built…

To every believer who's been publicly humiliated, privately shattered, and spiritually tested.

This is not your ending.

This is your **rebirth**.

This is your **vindication.**

This is what happens when the tears stop, the fire starts, and God steps in.

Now rise.

Speak.

Rebuild.

And rule.

Scriptures for Your Sealing Season:

- **Isaiah 61:7** – *"Instead of shame... double."*

- **Psalm 126:5** – *"Those who sow in tears shall reap in joy."*

- **Psalm 37:6** – *"He will bring forth your righteousness as the light, and your justice as the noonday."*

- **2 Samuel 22:49** – *"He brings me out from my enemies; He lifts me above those who rise against me..."*

- **Job 42:10** – *"And the Lord gave Job twice as much as he had before."*

Closing Charge:

Beloved, your reward is not coming — it is here.

Let the tears you cried become the oil you carry.

Let the betrayal become your building block.

Let the fire of the Holy Spirit burn everything that no longer belongs — and ignite everything God has ordained.

This is your vindication.

This is your get-back.

This is your God-fueled elevation.

The enemy took a lot…

But **Heaven gave you more**.

Now go, and don't ever apologize for the fire within you.

ABOUT THE AUTHOR

Her Excellency Ambassador Professor Dr. Onika Campbell-Rowe, D-CPC, D-MIN, Ph.D.

Global Motivational Speaker | Diplomat | Strategic Communication Leader | Humanitarian Trailblazer | Certified Life Coach | Author | International Educator. An Icon of Global Leadership and Humanitarian Impact

Her Excellency Ambassador Professor Dr. Onika Campbell-Rowe is a woman whose life and legacy transcend titles. She is a transformational leader, diplomatic voice of influence, and global force for good whose work has impacted nations, redefined communication in crisis, and elevated the lives of vulnerable communities across continents. With a professional journey spanning over two decades, Dr. Campbell-Rowe is internationally renowned as a motivational speaker, certified life coach, humanitarian strategist, academic, and communication analyst. Her influence stretches across diplomacy, education, public health, mental wellness, faith leadership, and sustainable development, making her one of the most decorated and dynamic women leaders of her generation.

A MISSION-DRIVEN GLOBAL VOICE

Dr. Campbell-Rowe's purpose is anchored in her personal mantra:

"Your story is not your end — it's your superpower." This conviction has guided her from the frontlines of humanitarian crisis response to the grand stages of **global summits**, **United Nations assemblies**, **faith-based missions**, and **academic institutions** around the world. Her speaking engagements are not mere presentations — they are **empowerment encounters**, blending strategic insight, emotional intelligence, and spiritual truth to uplift individuals, institutions, and societies.

Diplomatic Trailblazer & Strategic Communicator

As the **Director General of Communication and Information** for **WOLMI International Consulting Cabinet**, and **Main Representative to the United Nations in Vienna** for the **Canadian International Chaplaincy Association (CICA International)** — an NGO in Special Consultative Status with the **UN Economic and Social Council (ECOSOC)** — Dr. Campbell-Rowe leads **transformative diplomatic initiatives** that champion peace, gender equity, mental health access, and educational empowerment.

Her diplomatic contributions are further underscored by her tenure as **Honorary Consul of Jamaica to Antigua & Barbuda**, and by her senior roles in **government ministries, international agencies**, and **crisis communication task forces** where she has shaped public policy and strategic media narratives.

Academic Powerhouse & Educational Visionary

Dr. Campbell-Rowe's academic credentials reflect the **depth of her scholarship and the breadth of her expertise**:

- **Ph.D. in Journalism & International Relations** (Thames International University, Paris, France)
- **Doctor of Ministry & Christian Leadership (CICA International University and Seminary)**
- **Level 7 – Master's Advanced Diploma** in Health Care Skills UK (Clinical Leadership in Neurology)
- **Master of Diplomacy, Leadership, and Management**
- **Postgraduate Training** from UNFPA, WHO, PAHO, UNITAR & the UN Surgehub Global Surgery Learning Hub
- **Certified Strategic Leader and Manager (CSLM)**
- **Certified Professional Coach (D-CPC, FCPC)**

- **Full Professorship of International Negotiations and Strategic Leadership**

She currently serves as **Principal of the CICA University Technical Centre of Excellence, a City & Guilds Institute of London Accredited and Approved Centre**, and a **Full-time Professor at two universities**, advancing global access to education with an emphasis on **technical skills, public leadership, and psychological resilience.**

A Legacy of Recognition and Global Impact

Dr. Campbell-Rowe's unparalleled work in **diplomacy, humanitarian aid, education, communication, and public leadership** has earned her **over 20 prestigious global awards and recognitions**, including

- us **U.S. President's Lifetime Achievement Awards** (2022, 2023)
- Ghana Merit Awards –International Honors Class – Lifetime Achievement Awards
- **Global Human Rights Council Award for Peace & Sustainable Development** (2024)

- 🏅 **Global Impact Award** (2022)
- 🇯🇲 **Jamaican Diaspora Awards** – Music, Arts & Culture | Volunteerism | Humanitarian Service | Education Empowerment
- **PAHO/WHO Excellence in Journalism Awards** (2005, 2008)
- **National Humanitarian Award – ABGMA**
- **Commander of the Most Distinguished Orders:**
  - *Extraordinary Ambassadors (CSDE)*
  - *Special Envoys – Specialist in Journalism*
  - *Global Peace Ambassadors (CGPA)*
- **Fellow of the Most Excellent Order of International Experts (FOIE)**
- **MCGI Post-Nominal Member – Institute of London (Royal Charter)**
- **Indo-Asian Excellence Award** (2024)
- **City & Guilds London L6 & L7 Professional Recognition Awards**

Each award affirms her relentless dedication to empowering others and reshaping systems through compassion, knowledge, and advocacy.

A Voice That Heals, A Mind That Leads

As a **certified life coach**, Dr. Campbell-Rowe mentors youth, executives, clergy, humanitarian workers, and women in leadership, guiding them through **faith-aligned personal transformation**. Her speaking style is engaging, data-driven, and spiritually affirming, making her a **trusted keynote presence** in both secular and faith-based circles.

She has authored globally influential works, led mental health education in vulnerable regions, and contributed academic material to prestigious journals, including the *Routledge Handbook of Mental Disorders in the Caribbean and African Region*, with a focus on **neurological health, trauma care, and psychosocial resilience**.

Champion of Affordable Education

As Principal of the **CICA Technical Centre of Excellence**, Dr. Campbell-Rowe has overseen programs providing **95% scholarship-based tuition** to **over 900 international students**, many from underserved and conflict-affected backgrounds. Her model supports the **UN Sustainable Development Goals (SDGs)** with a focus on **Quality Education, Gender Equality, Health and Well-being, and Reduced Inequalities**.

Her academic innovation blends **technical education, emotional intelligence**, and **faith-based learning** into a holistic curriculum that prepares changemakers to lead with heart and skill.

The Movement Continues

H.E. Dr. Onika Campbell-Rowe is not simply a speaker — she is a **global movement**.

A movement for **healing through communication**.

A movement for **education as a human right**.

A movement for **diplomacy, gender equity, and purposeful leadership**.

Her voice resonates across cultures.

Her influence reforms systems.

And her legacy? **It's only just beginning.**

Other Works by the Author:

The Role of the Christian Wife to the Earthly Husbandman

A Helpmate, A Support to His Kind

A deeply spiritual exploration of the wife's divine calling — filled with prophetic wisdom, emotional healing, and kingdom perspective for women walking the path of partnership and purpose.

From the Black Sheep to the Palace

Story of Resilience and Early Struggles

An inspiring memoir of transformation from rejection to royal purpose. Dr. Onika Campbell-Rowe shares a gripping testimony of overcoming shame, betrayal, and isolation to walk boldly in destiny. A journey of faith, identity, and unshakable resilience.

For bookings, keynote engagements, partnerships, and consultations:

Email: onika.campbell@gmail.com   IG: Dr Onika Campbell-Rowe | Express Rhythm Collective –Harmony For Humanity | University Portal: https://cica-international.org/technical-centre-of-excellence